The W

Exposing the Subtlety of Satan

George Bloomer

Unless otherwise indicated, all Scripture quotations are taken from the *King James Version* of the Bible.

Copyright © 1999 by George Bloomer

Printed in the United States of America

All rights reserved. Written permission must be secured from publisher to use or reproduce any part of this book, except for brief quotations in critical reviews or articles.

ISBN: 1-892352-08-7

George Bloomer
PO Box 11563
Durham NC 27703

Contents

Foreword

Introduction

CHAPTER 1
The Witching Craft 11

CHAPTER 2
Rituals & Sexual Perversion 19

CHAPTER 3
Halloween: Worshiping the Horned God
With Tricks or Treats 31

CHAPTER 4
DTV (Demon TV):
Witchcraft in the Popular Media 35

CHAPTER 5
Satan Unmasked 51

CHAPTER 6
Generational Curses & Territorial Spirits 65

CHAPTER 7
Court Is In Session 77

CHAPTER 8
Destroying the Power of Witchcraft 87

Foreword

Over the years, Pastor George Bloomer has written about a variety of timely topics, including *warfare, demons and how they operate, and relationships*. Now he has written an enlightening and timely book entitled *The Witching Craft*. Pastor Bloomer's intense study of the subject combined with his many years of experience in ministry uniquely qualifies him to write about this important topic.

The book is written in a style that is easy to read and understand, and is full of scriptures to verify each point. Pastor Bloomer takes the reader back in history to learn the very roots of the demonic realm and then goes on to share his insight and revelation on how it is operating in the world today.

As Vice Presiding Bishop of P.A.W., I highly recommend this informative book. I believe readers will gain new insight into the dangers associated with the enemy and his evil agenda and will be better equipped to avoid the pitfalls of *The Witching Craft*.

Bishop Thomas Wesley Weeks Sr.

Introduction

In Acts chapter 8, a man by the name of Simon used sorcery to bewitch the people of Samaria. There are two spiritual realms in the earth, and Simon was an agent of Satan who did his "religious" bidding in the realm of the demonic. Simon was an agent of Satan's witching craft, and Samaria received him as a spiritual leader.

Because the demonic realm promotes error, most people who operate in that realm try to appear very "knowing" and "spiritual." Acts 8:9 tells us that Simon made this claim and used his deceptive power of sorcery over a community made up of 70,000 people in his first-century city. Verses 10 and 11 say that from the least unto the greatest of men, all gave heed unto Simon because of the length of time he had bewitched them.

But God had other plans for Samaria, so he sent them representatives from His spiritual realm.

> *But when they believed Philip preaching the things concerning the kingdom of God, and the name of Jesus Christ, they were baptized, both men and women. Then Simon himself believed also: and when he was baptized, he continued with Philip, and wondered, beholding the miracles and signs which were done* (Acts 8:12-13).

Simon went through the motions of salvation when, Phillip, Peter, and John interrupted his work in Samaria, but as the chapter continues, we see him receive this rebuke:

> *Thy money perish with thee, because thou hast thought that the gift of God may be purchased with*

> *money. Thou hast neither part nor lot in this matter: for thy heart is not right in the sight of God. Repent therefore of this thy wickedness, and pray God, if perhaps the thought of thine heart may be forgiven thee.*
>
> *For I perceive that thou art in the gall of bitterness, and in the bond of iniquity. Then answered Simon, and said, Pray ye to the Lord for me, that none of these things which ye have spoken come upon me* (Acts 8:20-24).

Here in God's Word, we see a classic confrontation of two conflicting spiritual realms that people have to deal with every day. God's realm of truth, and Satan's realm of error. And truth won out because Philip, Peter, and John not only knew but could demonstrate truth. If they hadn't been sent, error would have continued to reign in the Samaritan's hearts, just as it is reigning in America today. Because today the "Simon spirit" lives both in and out of Christ's church.

In America today, we are living in a generation that has been bewitched by Satan, and because he works his witching craft so well, only a few understand this. He works through generational/genealogical orders, the media, and of course through the deceptive orders and cults that practice his craft.

Satan sprinkles just enough truth over his poison to draw his victims, and many of God's children have bought into his lies and deceptions today in the church. His sorceries can come in many forms, and they can produce total destruction of peoples' lives. Emotional and mental breakdown, financial problems, and accident-proneness are just some of the curses Satan enslaves people with. And it all can start with something as seemingly innocent as a movie.

American movies and television have taught the deep things of witchcraft through slickly packaged productions and seemingly innocent cartoons since the early '30s. Halloween (a form of witchcraft) is celebrated annually in America, by thousands of people—both in and out of God's church. And there is currently a satanic coup brewing in the homes and churches of America while God's people sit back and do nothing to counter it.

In my previous book, *Witchcraft in the Pews*, I pointed out the exploding trend of witchcraft that has been blind-siding the church in America for years. In this book, *The Witching Craft*, I expose some of the history and practices of this dark delusion to hopefully shed a little more light on its deception. And I present the Bible's powerful truths of Christian authority over Satan's witching craft works.

It is my earnest desire that those who read this book will take control of any demonic situation in their lives because of the knowledge they find here, and that they will share this truth with others to help set them free also.

George Bloomer

1
The Witching Craft

Be not deceived; God is not mocked: for whatsoever a man soweth, that shall he also reap.

—Galatians 6:7

The subject of witchcraft is one Americans as a whole are very ignorant of. Some of our ignorance can be blamed on the secrecy involved in this ancient art. But much of it should go to the clergy of our day who aren't teaching Americans what the Word of God has to say on the subject. The acceptance of witchcraft in the city of Los Angeles has reached the point of appointing an official witch of the county. And many Americans around the country are turning to those who practice this art for solutions to daily problems. So, as I mentioned in my introduction, Simon the sorcerer lives.

To practice the witching craft, one must have some knowledge of astrology. So we will look at its beginnings in this book because modern witchcraft is nothing more than an advanced form of astrology. Human sacrifice, sexual degradation, homosexuality, and other vile practices are all part of this ancient art that birthed the witching craft.

To begin, let's define witchcraft. The word *witch* is derived from the Indo-European root word, *weik*, which means religion and magic. The word witchcraft comes from an old English term *wicce-craft*, which refers to the art or skill of using supernatural forces to bend the world to one's will. So witchcraft is a religion that worships Satan and his demonic forces in order to receive magic power to influence the wills of others. It is sometimes referred to as the religion of Wicca.

Witches pray to two main deities—the "queen" of the demon world, and the "horned god." In worshiping these deities, they look to different planets and stars that have been assigned to each deity.

For example, witchcraft worships the goddess Diana along with the planet Jupiter. Diana was the fertility goddess of the Ephesians and was worshiped in the idol form of a meteorite or stone. The Ephesians (Greeks) believed this stone came from the planet Jupiter, so Diana was sometimes called "mother earth," which means *fertility goddess;* thus the term "mother earth" became popularized.

This same goddess was called Ashtart by the Phoenicians and Asherah by the Canaanites. The English (Norse) worshiped this idol known to them by the name of Frigg. In fact, every nation in history practiced some form of witchcraft until the gospel of Jesus Christ reached their shores.

Death is glorified at various levels in the cult of witchcraft. In the beginning stages, one might begin by sacrificing frogs, cats, or birds. But the highest order of sacrifice is that of a human being. Through these killings, witches seek to please Satan's devils and to release his evil powers. Some in the craft even reach the point of sacrificing their own children to gain Satan's power.

Over the ages, positions and practices of the dark art have included:

- Divination—the practice of using the stars and evil spirits to foretell the future.
- Observers of times—A term used many times in the Bible, referring to astrology. In astrology, one observes

The Witching Craft

the movement of the sun, moon, stars, and planets to predict the future of man.

- Enchanter—One who casts spells upon people to control their actions.
- Witch—A woman enchanter who has great demonic powers.
- Charmer—A hypnotist who charms the mind and will of another person to gain control.
- Consulter with familiar spirits—A witch or enchanter who uses an animal to carry out an evil deed against another person.
- Wizard—One who uses magic and/or sorcery to control the wills of others.
- Necromancer—One who supposedly communicates with the dead.

All of these practices are condemned by God in Deuteronomy 18 and have at their root, evil deeds or death.

There is a story about a Swedish king by the name of Aun who sought to please the devil through the sacrificial offering of his sons. I think it makes a good point concerning Satan's unquenchable lust for death, which he employs in witchcraft to both serve and receive from him.

According to the story, this king had ten sons, but he had to sacrifice nine of them to the god of Odin in order to spare his own life.

After Aun sacrificed his second son, it is said the devil told him he would continue to live as long as he gave him another of his sons every ninth year.

When Aun sacrificed his seventh son, he was so feeble that he couldn't walk and had to be carried in a chair.

After he sacrificed his ninth son, he lived another nine years, but by then his health was so bad that he had to drink like a weaned baby.

Finally he sought to sacrifice his only remaining son, but as the story goes, the people of Sweden wouldn't let him do it. So the king finally died a murderer, and a very miserable man.

Oh, how weak Satan can make a man.

The Bible warns about such sacrifice as this legend attributes to Aun, because the eastern people of old commonly practiced them.

> *There shall not be found among you any one that maketh his son or his daughter to pass through the fire...* (Deuteronomy 18:10).

Astrology
A Most Ancient Path

Witchcraft's origins lie in astrology, which had its beginnings in the Tower of Babel in Genesis 11:

> *And the whole earth was of one language, and of one speech. And it came to pass, as they journeyed from the east, that they found a plain in the land of Shinar; and they dwelt there. And they said one to another, Go to, let us make brick, and burn them thoroughly. And they had brick for stone, and slime had they for mortar. And they said, Go to, let us build us a city and a tower, whose top may reach unto heaven; and let us make us a name, lest we be scattered abroad upon the face of the whole earth* (Genesis 11:1-4).

This infamous tower was built not long after Noah's flood, in what we refer to today as the modern nation of Iraq. It is important that we understand the Tower of Babel and its purpose because it stands at the beginning of the witching craft's arts.

The structure of this "high place" was discovered in 1876. In it was found a grand court 900 x 1,156 feet and a smaller one 450 x 1,056 feet, in which a walled-in platform was constructed that was surrounded by four gates on each side. In the center stood the tower with many shrines at its base, which obviously had been dedicated to various gods.

The tower itself was 300 feet high, with decreased width in stages from the lowest to the highest point. On its top rested a platform measuring 60 x 80 feet in width by 50 feet in height, on which was located a sanctuary for the god Belmerodach and signs of the zodiac. It was built for two main reasons:

1. To worship idol gods.

2. And to study the host of heaven (stars, moon, and planets).

In performing some of the rituals to the gods, sacrifices were made on the top of the tower. Much of this was done in secret, so the top of the tower provided the priest with a good place to carry out such acts. The tower's top also provided a primitive observatory for viewing the stars.

As previously mentioned, behind every group of stars was a god or goddess to be worshiped. It was for these reasons that God stepped in to stop the tower's construction and scattered the people around the earth.

After God destroyed the devil's worship, he scattered the people in different directions. Before the flood, the earth consisted of one land mass. So God split the earth into continents and islands (see Genesis 10:5-32). Once the earth was divided into nations, each had its own language, and many of them built their own towers to worship idol gods. The Egyptians built pyramids. So did the Aztec Indians of Mexico.

As history pushed on, the practices of the Babylonians were carried on by the Chinese, Indians, Romans, Greeks and to some extent, the Hebrews.

Following the flood, most of the world was engaged in astrological worship, paying fabricated homage to the solar system's planets and fabricated "gods."

It is said the ancient Egyptians built the Great Pyramid at Giza and its surrounding pyramids to reflect the constellation Orion, where they believed their kings ascended to become stars themselves after death.

In China, I-ching, with the principles of Ying and Yang (positive and negative energy forces produced by the stars), developed different rituals and games of chance to determine the fate of their followers.

In Daniel's Babylon, Nebuchadnezzar's soothsayer astrologers were consulted in matters of national welfare. The Chaldean caste system, briefly mentioned in Daniel's book, were of the highest social caste. Until they consulted the stars, no journey could begin, no building could be built, nor could any battle be undertaken.

The Persians who defeated Babylon in the sixth century B.C. continued the astrological practices of the Chaldean caste, and are said to have thought the stars they consulted were actually gods of the universe. Comets were believed to be the souls of good men on their way to heaven. And the Milky Way Galaxy was thought to be an old, unused path to the sun.

As the witching craft became more sophisticated, energy and the angular relationships of the planets were soon connected fatalistically in relation to the events of any given day or year. Natal charts, plotting which planets were where at the time of a person's birth, would soon act as manipulative factors to control a person's life.

The Magi, spoken of in the Matthew account of Jesus Christ's birth, are believed by many to have come from the Persian Chaldean caste where they had learned of Jehovah from exiled Jews. Others believe they were from Parthia. Regardless, their name, Magi, or *Magoi* in Greek, means "astrologer" and tells us they practiced magic or divination, including the consultation of the stars.

In fact, it was a star that brought the Magi to worship Jesus and give their gifts of gold, frankincense, and myrrh to Joseph and Mary (see Matthew 2:11). God apparently broke through their misguided system with a sign to make known to them the birth of His Son.

Wherever Christianity has changed a nation, awakened people have received the only true God. The many mystery cults Paul confronted in Rome all consulted their lucky stars according to their individual deities, until they heard the gospel. And that was once true in America.

Not too long ago, witchcraft, psychics, and fortunetellers were resigned in America to small, obscure city parlors and circus side shows. But this is not true today. Today in America, witchcraft and astrology have exploded around the media and across state lines. The only difference is our Babylonian towers are much more subtle in their deceptions and most commonly take the form of huge silver screens and 19" televisions. We will look at this closer in chapter four, but before we do, let's take a look at some of the witching craft's less subtle rituals that are as old as Satan himself.

2
Rituals & Sexual Perversion

> *...Be not deceived: neither fornicators, nor idolators, nor adulterers, nor effeminate, nor abusers of themselves with mankind...shall inherit the kingdom of God.*
> —1 Corinthians 6:9,10

Rituals are far more important to Satan than they are to our Living God. Why? Because pomp and circumstance provides him one of the few acts of faith his followers can demonstrate. Rituals also provide a launching site for the devil, allowing him to work those he deceives into a frenzy and causing them to act out his devilish will.

The highest of Satan's rituals are those that involve murder—the sacrifice of human lives offered in exchange for his approval and power. Some of these rituals involve the casting of demonic spells.

There is an herb used in some witchcraft killing rituals known as "Adam and Eve." This herb is used in casting spells. "Adam and Eve" is a very poisonous and deadly plant that is said to turn milk as clear as water within twenty-four hours. Its name is derived from the fact that when the roots are placed in water, its tiny peanut-like roots separate, with some rising to the top and the others sinking to the bottom. Witches say this is the separation of the male and female and that the female part of the root rises to the top. Those who are tricked or seduced into drinking this deadly poison die as a satanic sacrifice in the witching craft's deadly cause.

Sexual Perversion in Worship

Sexual perversion is also an integral part of the witching craft's rituals. Witches worship both gods and goddesses according to the seasons of the year. Witchcraft goddesses are usually worshiped during spring and summer, while their gods are worshiped during fall and winter. The belief behind this is that the female gives birth to life, which is produced in the spring and summer months. It is for this reason that many goddesses are referred to as Mother Nature, or Mother Earth. Mother Earth for the Ephesians in biblical times was Diana. For the Phoenicians she was Ashtart. And for the English (Norse), she was Frigg.

In the Canaanite culture, the symbol of Asherah (Ashtart) was a wooden pole. The pole was symbolic of life, generations, and fertilizing power. It was sometimes referred to as the tree of life. From these concepts and views of their gods and goddesses, it isn't difficult to see why their views of sexuality would be perverted. In some countries, special holidays were set aside to worship these goddesses, at which time women would sell their bodies to raise funds for the temple.

In Babylon, a woman had to prostitute herself once during her lifetime in the temple of Venus. Once inside the temple, no woman could leave until she had paid her debt and deposited on the altar of the goddess the funds received for her sexual acts. Every woman was religiously charged with an arbitrary debt. A young and beautiful woman might spend as much as three years in the temple.

It was also the custom on certain days for Satan's high priest to have sexual relations with all the women before planting time. This was done to insure a fertile crop during the year. The priest used an artificial phallus (male sex organ) made of stone in the shape and size of the male organ. The women endured this act because they believed it would cause their families to have an abundant crop.

Rituals & Sexual Perversion

In other nations, on the night of a full moon, a man and his wife would go to a planting field before it was sown, to engage in sexual relations. This ritual was carried out in the belief that it to would cause bigger yields.

The corruption of pagan immorality eventually destroyed the nation of Israel from within. Its influence is seen early in the Book of Exodus when Moses came down off the mount.

> *And it came to pass, as soon as he came nigh unto the camp, that he saw the calf, and the dancing: and Moses' anger waxed hot, and he cast the tables out of his hands, and brake them beneath the mount. And he took the calf which they had made, and burnt it in the fire, and ground it to powder, and strowed it upon the water, and made the children of Israel drink of it.*
>
> *And Moses said unto Aaron, What did this people unto thee, that thou hast brought so great a sin upon them? And Aaron said, Let not the anger of my lord wax hot: thou knowest the people, that they are set on mischief. For they said unto me, Make us gods, which shall go before us: for as for this Moses, the man that brought us up out of the land of Egypt, we wot not what is become of him. And I said unto them, Whosoever hath any gold, let them break it off. So they gave it me: then I cast it into the fire, and there came out this calf.*
>
> *And when Moses saw that the people were naked; (for Aaron had made them naked unto their shame among their enemies:) then Moses stood in the gate of the camp, and said, Who is on the Lord's side? let him come unto me. And all the sons of Levi gathered themselves together unto him* (Exodus 32:19-26).

Many were put to death by the sword on that day by the Levites, who obeyed God's command to destroy those involved with this nakedness at the foot of the mount.

In Deuteronomy we find:

> *There shall be no whore of the daughters of Israel, nor a sodomite of the sons of Israel. Thou shall not bring the hire of a whore or the price of a dog, into the house of the Lord thy God for any vow: for even both these are abomination unto the Lord thy God* (Deuteronomy 23:17,18).

Israel's death knell as a people was spoken in 2 Chronicles 28:

> *For the Lord brought Judah low because of Ahaz king of Israel; for he made Judah naked, and transgressed sore against the Lord* (2 Chronicles 28:19).

So this basest form of witchcraft is certainly nothing to wink at. It can destroy whole nations when allowed to go unchecked.

In Paul's day, such acts were so common that it was a part of their daily worship. So he continually warned the people concerning their culture's immoral customs:

> *Know ye not that the unrighteous shall not inherit the kingdom of God? Be not deceived: neither fornicators, nor idolaters, nor adulterers, nor effeminate, nor abusers of themselves with mankind, nor thieves, nor covetous, nor drunkards, nor revilers, nor extortioners, shall inherit the kingdom of God. And such were some of you: but ye are washed, but ye are sanctified, but ye are justified in the name of the Lord Jesus, and by the Spirit of our God...Now the body is not for fornication, but for the Lord; and the Lord for the body* (1 Corinthians 6:9-11,13).

Rituals & Sexual Perversion

Homosexuality

And they have cast lots for my people; and have given a boy for an harlot, and sold a girl for wine, that they might drink (Joel 3:3).

Homosexuality is one of the most wicked and dehumanizing acts that a man can commit, and its roots run deep in astrology and witchcraft.

You won't find the word *homosexual* in the Bible. But you will find the word s*odomite*, which is essentially the same thing. When you study the origins of homosexuality, you will find yourself reading about the ancient city of Sodom. This city can probably be called the "cradle of homosexuality." It was there that the word "sodomy" developed, and it was there that the widespread indulgence in this vile act took root.

We read of Lot's encounter with the vile perverts of this city in Genesis 19:

But before they lay down, the men of the city, even the men of Sodom, compassed the house round, both old and young, all the people from every quarter: and they called unto Lot, and said unto him, Where are the men which came in to thee this night? bring them out unto us, that we may know them (have sex with them). *And Lot went out at the door unto them, and shut the door after him, and said, I pray you, brethren, do not so wickedly* (vvs. 4-7).

The passage goes on to reveal Lot's offering of his daughters to Sodom's homosexual men, and that the angels the men were demanding struck these perverts blind. Why such vile behavior? How did they become such wicked men? Let us look at Paul's revelation to more fully sort it out.

Paul's address to the Romans on this subject makes God's views of the perversion very plain. When men and women burn in lust for one another, there is a degrading of God's creation that twists the thinking process in such a way that carnal appetite can overrule the rational thinking process.

> *Professing themselves to be wise, they became fools, and changed the glory of the uncorruptible God into an image made like to corruptible man, and to birds, and fourfooted beasts, and creeping things. Wherefore God also gave them up to uncleanness through the lusts of their own hearts, to dishonour their own bodies between themselves: who changed the truth of God into a lie, and worshipped and served the creature more than the Creator, who is blessed forever. Amen.*
>
> *For this cause God gave them up unto vile affections: for even their women did change the natural use into that which is against nature: and likewise also the man, leaving the natural use of the woman, burned in their lust one toward another; men with men working that which is unseemly, and receiving in themselves that recompense of their error which was meet* (Romans 1:22-27).

One other hideous example of this basest fruit of witchcraft can be found in Judges 19. It almost parallels the situation in Sodom. In this case, a group of Hebrew homosexuals demanded sex with a visitor in their city, and the incident ended in the murder of a woman who was given over to them:

> *Now as they were making their hearts merry, behold, the men of the city, certain sons of Belial, beset the house round about, and beat at the door, and spake to the master of the house, the old man saying, Bring forth the man that came into thine house, that we may know him. And the man, the master of the house, went out unto them, and said unto them, Nay, my brethren, nay, I pray you do not so wickedly; seeing that this man is come into mine house, do not this folly. Behold, here is my daughter*

a maiden, and his concubine; them I will bring out now, and humble ye them, and do with them what seemeth good unto you: but unto this man do not so vile a thing.

But the men would not hearken to him; so the man took his concubine, and brought her forth unto them; and they knew her, and abused her all the night until the morning: and when the day began to spring, they let her go. Then came the woman in the dawning of the day, and fell down at the door of the man's house where her lord was, till it was light.

And her lord rose up in the morning, and opened the doors of the house, and went out to go his way: and, behold, the woman his concubine was fallen down at the door of the house, and her hands were upon the threshold. And he said unto her, Up, and let us be going. But none answered. Then the man took her up upon an ass, and the man rose up, and gat him unto his place. And when he was come into his house, he took a knife and laid hold on his concubine and divided her, together with her bones, into twelve pieces, and sent her into all the coasts of Israel.

And it was so, that all that saw it said, There was no such deed done nor seen from the day that the children of Israel came up out of the land of Egypt unto this day: consider of it, take advice, and speak your minds (Judges 19:22-30).

There is a perverse immoral spirit that confuses and debases in homosexuality. The spirit was given such free reign in both Sodom and Gibeah that the men afflicted with it thought nothing of murdering any who would not submit to their rape. Law and social resistance has restrained that level of lawlessness in America today—but just watch some of the footage from San Francisco's Gay Pride Parade, and you will see an alarming circus of sensual debauchery that offends rational thought. Though their "agenda" has ensured press coverage of their "coming out" events, you won't see most of what takes place at this parade in any TV report because it's too obscene to air on network television.

The Sodomite In Pagan Worship

He that is wounded in the stones, or hath his privy member cut off, shall not enter into the congregation of the Lord...There shall be no whore of the daughters of Israel, nor a sodomite of the sons of Israel. Thou shall not bring the hire of a whore, or the price of a dog, into the house of the Lord thy God for any vow: for even both these are abomination unto the Lord thy God (Deuteronomy 23:1,17,18).

As we have seen, heathen nations erected temples to their gods and goddesses, in which sexual sacrifices were offered to idols because sex was a form of worship. As previously mentioned, women paid their vows to the temple by prostituting themselves for money, which was left in the temple. In other temples, males or sodomites were assigned to perform homosexual acts. Sodomites were males—many who were given to the service of the gods—who had been subjected to the removal of their genitalia so that their only means of sexual pleasure was homosexuality. The men of the city would visit the temple, perform sexual acts with other men, and leave money to support the temple. They believed their union with a sodomite represented communion with the horned god and that the sodomite served as a contact with that god. This practice was so widespread throughout the Gentile nations that the Jews referred to all Gentiles as dogs. The term "dog" is used because this sexual act is performed in the same manner as dogs.

Make no mistake regarding this issue—it is an abomi tion to the Lord. And God commands man to abhor hom. sexual acts:

Thou shalt not lie with mankind, as with womankind: it is abomination (Leviticus 18: 22).

If a man also lie with mankind, as he lieth with a woman, both of them have committed an abomination: they shall surely be put to death; their blood shall be upon them (Leviticus 20:13).

Bestiality

Thou shalt not lie with mankind, as with womankind...Neither shalt thou lie with any beast to defile thyself therewith: neither shall any woman stand before a beast to lie down thereto: it is confusion (Leviticus 18:22,23).

To take sexual perversion down yet another step, Satan's immoral degradation incorporates witchcraft rituals of human sex with animals. In the craft, certain animals are believed to be used by the devil to manifest himself. The goat is symbolic of Satan, so in some rituals, women have relations with a goat to increase their powers to cast spells.

The witchcraft practice of beastiality is so abominable in God's sight that He condemned both together in Exodus 22:

Thou shall not suffer a witch to live. Whosoever lieth with a beast shall surely be put to death (Exodus 22:18,19).

The Sensual '90s

What many called the "Sexual Revolution" that exploded in the '60s, was incorporated into the religions of Paul's day.

What some are calling the "Gay Agenda" of the '80s was called sodomy and was judged with fire and brimstone in Abraham's day. And one would have to be blind not to see how witchcraft's immoral influence has flooded the '90s of today.

The reason there is so much child pornography in the world today, is because there is so much witchcraft in the world today. Sensuality causes men to live in a state of nudity and immorality that demands lewder and more debased acts to fulfill its passions. Paul wrote of such rebels in Romans, chapter 1:

> *Being filled with all unrighteousness, fornication, wickedness, covetousness, maliciousness; full of envy, murder, debate, deceit, malignity; whisperers, backbiters, haters of God, despiteful, proud, boasters, inventors of evil things, disobedient to parents, without understanding, covenantbreakers, without natural affection, implacable, unmerciful: who knowing the judgment of God, that they which commit such things are worthy of death, not only do the same, but have pleasure in them that do them* (Romans 1:29-32).

The more sensuous a person is, the more of their body—and others' bodies—they want to see and show. The flood of infectious diseases caused by immorality's spread throughout today's world has certainly presented man with a telltale sign. But there is a satanic spirit behind all of it that rejects the effects seen. AIDS has even been given a political status that rejects its root homosexual cause.

Consider the evils of homosexuality—then take the advice of Paul and help any you know to turn from the practice of such perverting acts that lead to the destruction of society.

Remember:
- God destroyed the city of Sodom because of this sin.

- The waters of the Dead Sea cover this former city today.
- The Dead Sea has no life in it (fish, plants, frogs, etc.)
- The Dead Sea covering Sodom is at the lowest point on the face of the earth.

When I consider these truths, I am led to believe that when man engages in the sin of homosexuality, it lowers him to the lowest of morals.

Original Sin

In completing this chapter, a very basic yet important question we must ask is: "Where did Satan get this power to deceive and enslave huge populations?"

The answer is: from God Almighty.

Next we might ask, "Why does God continue to allow the devil to have such power?"

Perhaps the best way to reach an understanding of these questions is to refer to Adam and Eve's transgression in Genesis 2:16,17:

And the Lord God commanded the man, saying, Of every tree of the garden thou mayest freely eat: but of the tree of the knowledge of good and evil, thou shalt not eat of it: for in the day that thou eatest thereof thou shalt surely die.

We all know that Adam and Eve ate from this tree of the knowledge of good and evil. And because they did, we their offspring must also learn the lessons of good and evil. And since God is good and there is no evil in Him (see James 1:13,17), He has allowed the devil to continue to exist to show us the difference between good and evil to help us make a proper choice:

See, I have set before thee this day life and good, and death and evil...I call heaven and earth to

> *record this day against you, that I have set before you life and death, blessing and cursing: therefore choose life, that both thou and thy seed may live* (Deuteronomy 30:15,19).

Although Satan has power, the Book of Job reveals that he must check with God before he can attack us (see Job 1:6-12). So we should always remember that Satan's power is limited...and even more so in his demon servants. But neither should we forget that our authority as children of God is determined by our knowledge of God's Word.

Today, the lust levels within the church are at an all-time high because very few people are preaching on the reality of demonic interaction, especially in the area of sensuality. Sensuality or "impurity" is listed among the works of the flesh in Galatians 5:19, and has always been one of Satan's greatest threats to the church. Just read about the immorality problems that existed in the seven first-century churches in Revelation, and you can date the New Testament problem. And if you were to receive an honest response to any poll in any church, you would find a number of strongholds that need to be destroyed.

Satan promotes himself today under many attractive titles that American airwaves carry twenty-four hours a day, all of which have their deceptive roots in Genesis 11. As we will see in coming chapters, most of these evil crafts have been spoon-fed to many as fairytales and entertainment that subtly plant Satan's ideas of witchcraft in theaters and homes.

In the next chapter, we will look at the most popular witchcraft ritual ever: Halloween. It is a witching craft celebration that Satan has packaged with costumes, parties, free candy, and "fun"...all to glorify death.

3
Halloween:
Worshiping the Horned God With Tricks or Treats

There shall not be found among you any one that maketh his son or his daughter to pass through the fire...

—Deuteronomy 18:10

Halloween, or All Hallows Eve, is probably the most overt demonstration of witchcraft in the western world today. It has become an annual event in America, and many of us take part in the celebration. We buy masks and costumes, cut faces into pumpkins, and give candy to children. But how many of us really know the true origin and meaning of the celebration?

In witchcraft, there are four main sabbaths of feast day, but Halloween is the most important. The word means *holy evening.* So Halloween *is Satan's holy evening.*

Halloween's sabbath, which is observed every October 31st, represents the end of summer and the beginning of winter; the end of life and the beginning of death. Remember, in pagan worship, their gods and goddesses are worshiped by the seasons of the year. The goddesses represent life and are worshiped spring through fall. The horned god that is referred to as "the god of the dead" is worshiped in the winter. This is what Halloween is truly all about—the worship of the dead.

Trick or Treat

This custom comes to us from the Irish Druids. Those involved in the practice of witchcraft would make a journey to their festival honoring the dead. On their way, they would stop at the doors of the houses they passed to obtain food for their trip. If they were given food that pleased them, they would bless that house. If they were refused food or didn't like what was given to them, they would cast spells on that house.

Masks and Costumes

This custom is also from the Celtic and Irish Druids. It was the custom to gather around their bonfires to offer sacrifices. Many times they would wear the skins and heads of animals. They believed the horned god would manifest himself through those who wore the head of a goat. And those who wore goat masks would tell the fortunes of their friends and neighbors for the coming year. According to Satan's witching craft, Halloween is the best time of the year to consult the stars concerning the future.

Jack-o'-Lantern

The lighted pumpkin face of the jack-o'-lantern is the ancient symbol for a damned soul that is doomed to wander until Judgment Day. Its tradition came about from an old legend about Jack, an Irish alcoholic who pleaded with the devil to share one last drink with him when he came to claim his soul. As the story goes, the devil agreed, and Jack conned the devil into paying for the drink by turning himself into a coin. Then once Satan was transformed, Jack put him into his wallet that had a cross on it, thus trapping him inside because of the cross.

So Satan agreed to let Jack live ten more years, and he was freed from the wallet. Then when Satan returned for him, Jack convinced the devil to climb a tree and bring him an apple. But Jack tricked him again—this time by carving a cross in the tree and forcing the devil to stay up there because he couldn't come near the cross. So once again the devil agreed to let him live. So Jack removed the cross, and the devil went on his way.

Finally, the legend concludes, when Jack died as a wicked old man and went to hell, Satan wouldn't let him in. So Jack requested a light to find his way back to earth through the darkness, and he was given a turnip and a burning coal to make a lantern. As the tradition grew, pumpkins replaced turnips in their Halloween representations, and the jack-o'-lantern, a symbol of the dead finding their way back to earth, was witchingly birthed.

An Ancient Path

I have found in my many studies that the worship of the dead is a universal trend in the worshiping of idols. The practice of honoring the dead was observed by the Persians, Chinese, American Indians, Assyrians, British, Irish, Scots, and many other nations. Many of these traditions believe the spirits of good men are taken by angels to paradise and the spirits of evil men are left to wander some place between the earth and heaven. They also hold that the spirits of the wicked return on Halloween to their former homes to be entertained by the living.

Many other rituals have been carried out over the years to appease the horned god and to avoid the torment of the dead's returning spirits. They include:

Human Sacrifices

Huge bonfires were built on hilltops, and live people—usually prisoners— were placed into the fire in wicker boxes. In some cases, participants would even place their own firstborn children into the fire. Following the sacrifice, worshipers would throw stones with their names engraved on them into the fire. They would return the next day to hopefully dig their stones from the ashes. If their stone was found, it meant they would live to see another Halloween. But if it was lost, it served as an omen of their impending death before the next Halloween.

We as Americans have been led to believe there is no harm in celebrating Halloween. But as you should now see, its festivities are meant to serve and glorify Satan. These wicked customs came to America in the late nineteenth century with the influence of the Irish, but they are the practices of heathens meant to serve Satan's evil end.

> *When thou art come into the land which the Lord thy God giveth thee, thou shalt not learn to do after the abominations of those nations. There shall not be found among you any one that maketh his son or his daughter to pass through the fire, or that useth divination, or an observer of times, or an enchanter, or a witch* (Deuteronomy 18:9,10).

In the next chapter, we will look at how the witching craft's practices have been polished and packaged by television and Hollywood to enslave both adults and children, under the guise of "fun."

4
DTV:
(Demon TV)
Witchcraft in the Popular Media

For all that do these things are an abomination unto the LORD: and because of these abominations the LORD thy God doth drive them out from before thee.

—Deuteronomy 18:12

In my travels around the world, I've seen witchcraft in many places—but I have to say there is more witchcraft practiced in America than in any other country on the face of the earth.

When public school teachers give your children trolls with funny hairdos and stomach charms to play with and tell them to wish upon them, they're teaching your children witchcraft. When they teach them mental telepathy's power to leave their young minds and enter another person's telepathically, this is also witchcraft.

Distribution of government-sponsored condoms shows witchcraft's influence of immorality at the highest level, and abortion is nothing less than a form of witchcraft's sacrificial death. Remember, Satan is the author of death, and he will influence anyone he can so he can be glorified through it.

The Witching Craft

Witchcraft Central—USA

Without a doubt, *the* most effective method of instruction Satan has been able to manipulate in imparting his witching craft message into modern society has been through movies and television. Americans have become cultivated by Hollywood's witching stories because of their entertaining qualities. But behind the scenes, unseen by most, many are drawn into witchcraft's darkness because of the influence of film. What appears "laughable" fun and superstition to some, becomes religion to others.

Walt Disney Studios began the "dumbing down" process in 1937 with its heartwarming portrayal of "Snow White and the Seven Dwarfs," a sweet, loving maiden who was murdered through witchcraft, then raised from the dead. They surrounded Snow White with funny dwarfs and cuddly animals, but the wicked queen who transformed herself into a hideous witch frightened young eyes until the film's happy end.

The cartoon's wicked queen's mirror spoke back through a familiar spirit. And the only reason Snow White escaped her plotted murder was because the one assigned to kill her and *cut out her heart* was too soft-hearted to fulfill the queen's command.

Magic spells set the theme of "Cinderella" (1950), but because of its enchanting presentation, the reality of its witchcraft overtones are glossed over. The film's funny little mice and moving music distract from the message at its core. However, if you watch some of the film's young viewers (it's been re-released in theaters and on video), you may notice some of them playing around with the casting of spells. And if you ask them their playtime purpose in doing so, they will tell you their magic is meant for good—because good overcomes evil. And they will tell you that Cinderella's fairy godmother was a force of good. But as "Zipedee Bobidee" comes out of their mouths, Satan is watching for those little ones who will

DTV (Demon TV): Witchcraft in the Popular Media

eventually believe it. No, I don't mean he has any power to manifest this or that, but he is watching for those young ones who may be ready for his next level of deception.

Now, Walt Disney has produced many more productions involving witchcraft than I will be listing here, but the few I am bringing up have become a part of American culture because of their success.

In Disney's "Sleeping Beauty" (1959), a princess is cursed by a witch, who declares in her evil pronouncement that the princess will die before her sixteenth birthday by the prick of a poisoned spinning wheel needle. The curse proves lethal, and this innocent woman—like Snow White—also falls into a deathly state until she too is raised from the dead.

And what of Mickey? Mickey Mouse's blockbuster role as the "Sorcerer's Apprentice" in the highly acclaimed cartoon "Fantasia" (1940), showed the cute creature waving his wand and casting spells that produced drug-like-induced apparitions, including Satan and hell.

It is not my intention to pin a satanic agenda on Hollywood as a whole. However, because Satan's highest form of deception is through innocent entrapment, I believe the majority in Hollywood look at witching tales as moneymaking products. Most are ignorant of the devil's deeper, hidden cause. But I also believe there are those involved in scripting who specifically research to magnify Satan and even recruit for his cause.

There is No Such Thing As a Good Witch

One historic cause that certainly bears mentioning is Hollywood's incessant attempt at dividing Satan's kingdom into good and bad dominions with good and bad witches. The lovable fairy godmother in Cinderella who cast spells and changed Cinderella's natural circumstances certainly wasn't an angel. She was a spirit being who appeared out of nowhere, cast spells with her words, and was just a little scatterbrained for humorous effect.

But there is no such thing as a "good" witch. Anyone in the craft who attains the level of actually becoming one, doesn't arrive there because of a drive to do good.

Remember Samantha the "good" witch and her "bad" witch mother Endora on the popular '60s sitcom "Bewitched"? It was this TV series that made witchcraft look respectable in an American suburban home. And Samantha's good witchcraft always won out with a wiggle of her nose or an appeal to her evil mom. I'll talk more about this program later because of its amazing long-running influence in bringing common witchcraft practices into American homes.

The number one witchcraft movie ever made, "The Wizard of Oz" (1939), probably did more for Satan's lie of good and bad witches than any production in history. Remember, it was filled with witches and goblins, and even had the name *wizard* in its title. Every American in my generation who owned an old black and white or new color TV has seen it multiple times. And now it is out on video so parents can impart their cultural experience on "family video night." But it is shot through with potions, spells, and demons.

The main character in this witching tale, Dorothy of Kansas, has a dream in which she goes "over the rainbow" into Munchkin Land. Fairytale lore calls Munchkins dwarfs and trolls, but they are actually demonic figures. Websters Dictionary defines them as "short demon-like creatures that live in dungeons or under bridges."

The main plot of the picture involves two bad witches—the wicked witch of the east and the wicked witch of the west. And it involves a good witch, Glenda, who arrives in the picture looking just like Cinderella's fairy godmother, with wand in hand and royal garb. Dorothy, who comes out of the north, kills the wicked witch of the east when her house falls out of the sky. Not long after, the good witch from the south hears of the news and pops up on the scene.

Now, notice that the first thing Glenda asks Dorothy is, "Are you a good or a bad witch?" From then on, the entire program is made up of murderous plots, spells, and demon-like monkeys that are controlled by the wicked witch of the west. The plot surrounds the witch's magic, which is worked on Dorothy and her gang to kill them and obtain a pair of magic slippers.

So again we have an innocent young woman at odds with the forces of satanic evil. And because it is very entertaining, the movie seems to deal with a fairytale world. But it actually deals with witchcraft in a very compelling way.

At the very least, "The Wizard of Oz" has given hundreds of thousands of children demon-monkey nightmares over the decades that it has aired on TV. At the very most, it has taught American viewers about spells, demon activity, fear, and deception. And more than any other movie, it has sold the deceptive notions of "good witches" to movie fans.

Jesus said a tree is known by its fruit (see Matthew 7:17). Therefore, to claim good witches, is to claim good demons—and to claim good demons, is to claim Satan as good. This is the agenda.

Bewitched

Now let's talk a little about the long-running television program (going on forty years now with reruns and cable), "Bewitched." And to start the discussion, we will refer to a witchcraft story that took place in the life of Israel's first king, Saul.

When Saul lost his favor with God, he sought to somehow manipulate God's will. And in one of his attempts, he contacted the witch of Endor to bring up the dead spirit of Samuel to hopefully receive good news:

> Then said Saul unto his servants, Seek me a woman that hath a familiar spirit, that I may go to her, and inquire of her. And his servants said to him, Behold, there is a woman that hath a familiar spirit at Endor. And Saul disguised himself, and put on other raiment, and he went, and two men with him, and they came to the woman by night: and he said, I pray thee, divine unto me by the familiar spirit, and bring me him up, whom I shall name unto thee. And the woman said unto him, Behold, thou knowest what Saul hath done, how he hath cut off those that have familiar spirits, and the wizards, out of the land: wherefore then layest thou a snare for my life, to cause me to die? And Saul sware to her by the Lord, saying, As the Lord liveth, there shall no punishment happen to thee for this thing.
>
> Then said the woman, Whom shall I bring up unto thee? And he said, Bring me up Samuel. And when the woman saw Samuel, she cried with a loud voice: and the woman spake to Saul, saying, Why hast thou deceived me? for thou art Saul. And the king said unto her, Be not afraid: for what sawest thou? And the woman said unto Saul, I saw gods ascending out of the earth. And he said unto her, What form is he of? And she said, An old man cometh up; and he is covered with a mantle. And Saul perceived that it was Samuel, and he stooped with his face to the ground, and bowed himself. And Samuel said to Saul, Why hast thou disquieted me, to bring me up? And Saul answered, I am sore distressed; for the Philistines make war against me, and God is departed from me, and answereth me no more, neither by prophets, nor by dreams: therefore

> *I have called thee, that thou mayest make known unto me what I shall do.*
>
> *Then said Samuel, Wherefore then dost thou ask of me, seeing the Lord is departed from thee, and is become thine enemy? And the Lord hath done to him, as he spake by me: for the Lord hath rent the kingdom out of thine hand, and given it to thy neighbour, even to David: Because thou obeyedst not the voice of the Lord, nor executedst his fierce wrath upon Amalek, therefore hath the Lord done this thing unto thee this day. Moreover the Lord will also deliver Israel with thee into the hand of the Philistines: and to morrow shalt thou and thy sons be with me: the Lord also shall deliver the host of Israel into the hand of the Philistines.*
>
> *Then Saul fell straightway all along on the earth, and was sore afraid, because of the words of Samuel: and there was no strength in him; for he had eaten no bread all the day, nor all the night* (1 Samuel 28:7-20).

In this seance account, Saul actually went into the country of Endor to find a witch with a familiar spirit to conjure up the dead. And when he did, she brought up an apparition that appeared before him. Whether it was actually Samuel or not is argued in theological circles, but it did come up, and it talked with Saul.

Now, do you remember the name of Samantha's "wicked witch" mother who used to regularly cast spells on her daughter's mortal husband Darin in "Bewitched"? Her name was Endora—taken from the land of Saul's witch—and she engaged in levitation, incantations, and supernatural transformations in program episodes. So did her "good witch" daughter Samantha—that is, when she was forced to work her magic for "good."

Kashaph is the Hebrew word for *witch*, which means, "to whisper a spell, i.e. to inchant or practice magic." It is also translated *sorcerer* as it is applied to witchcraft. When Samantha forgot certain spells because she had distanced herself from evil, she would have to put her memory to work. But when she did—Whammm!—magic exploded in the Steven's house.

Not only that, but the program gave witchcraft a sense of superiority and supernatural god-like qualities that only Hollywood could provide. Samantha's evil relatives lived on another plane of immortality, from where they looked down on mere mortals as if humans were unevolved weaklings. This is how Satan thinks of himself and his fallen kingdom. So remember—when we are shown things on television, it's often not by mistake.

The Importance of Guarding the "Eye-Gate"

Demon possession was thrust upon America's media-conscious society in 1973 with the Academy Award winning movie, "The Exorcist," in which a young girl's possession transformed her voice and physical appearance. Other movies since then have presented Satan's less-subtle agenda by capitalizing on what most would only refer to as *horror* movies. But most of them have at their core at least some demonic truth.

One movie in particular, "Poltergeist," like "Ghost," incorporated a medium to exorcise a family's house that was being "haunted" by the disembodied spirits of an Indian graveyard. The interaction between the two realms was fictional. But again, who knows which viewers watching this movie—and its sequence versions—were actually drawn into the demonic realm? Who knows which ones were so frightened by its presentation of demonic apparitions that their fears presented an actual door into the demonic realm?

DTV (Demon TV): Witchcraft in the Popular Media

We take these things for granted in America—and again I could be accused of making mountains out of molehills—but what we so often take for granted concerning what we let into our "eye-gates," can cause certain people both emotional and spiritual pain.

Why do small children have nightmares after watching so-called "horror" movies? And why don't you let your small ones watch them? Think about it.

Many other popular television programs have aired since the '60s that started teaching the deep things of Satan incrementally in an "entertaining" way.

A large number of horror-based programs such as "Tales from the Crypt," dealt with witchcraft in a horror show vein with vampires and ghouls. But there was one program that aired in American homes during the late '60s that probably did more to open America's general understanding to witchcraft than any other program. It was called "Night Gallery," and it dealt with authentic beliefs and practices of the witching craft. Solstice rituals, spells, incantations, and demonic entrapment were all portrayed in varying scripts of this weekly production. And as the program developed a following, a flood of pentagram-covered books suddenly appeared on American bookshelves.

The writer of the popular Saturday morning "Smurfs" cartoon program, which aired for seven years in the late '70s and early '80s, admitted that he took time to read the satanic scriptures by Antwan Devain to receive his inspiration.

One of the main program figures, Gargamell, was a warlock who wore a witchcraft pentagram symbol around his neck and cast spells. Gargamell's cat was named Asrelle. In my study of different occult names, I learned that Asrelle was the name of an avenging angel of Satan. The cat's mission in the program? To kill the Smurfs because he was the avenging death angel of Gargamell.

The Witching Craft

In fact, the Smurf's writer—who divulged his program objectives to the 700 Club after he received Jesus Christ as Savior and Lord—admitted that every one of his Smurf characters were developed with witchcraft in mind. One of his characters, named Vanity (meaning pleasures) was neither male or female—and America's children have grown up with this.

"He-man, Master of the Universe" established an incredible marketing craze of action figures and accessories involving a character who received supernatural powers from "Gray Scull," whose name and presence personified and glorified death. So in this program, the witching agenda came out a little clearer in young minds. And if you keep on hearing a thing—whether it be true or false—you will believe a lie before you believe the truth.

"Teenage Mutant Ninja Turtles" also broke into the movies and their action figures are still being sold. What could be so bad about four humorous half-shelled turtles running around kicking and fighting, seemingly having fun? Well, first of all, these reptilian figures are part of the Bhuddist pagan religion known as *Zen*. In one Ninja episode, a rat god is their leader that gets caught. One of the Turtles, Leonardo, practices mental telepathy to contact the rat. When he locates him telepathically, his turtle chums gather around a bon- or bell-fire, which is a practice of witchcraft. Then one of the Ninja "good guys" congratulates Leonardo for his telepathic success and says, "You have done well. You have completed your life study. You have become an "I am." This is basic Bhuddism.

Buddhism teaches that you are god, as does Hinduism. The entire series revolves around these hero turtles fighting the forces of evil in the name of becoming "gods." Of course, it is veiled within all of the "kung fu-ing" and entertainment.

DTV (Demon TV): Witchcraft in the Popular Media

Magic

Back to Disney. Walt Disney's production house is called the *Magic Kingdom.* Notice the word "magic." There is nothing noble or good about the word magic. It is actually an occult word that applies to Satan's dark powers. And again, there is no good (white) and evil (black) magic. It is all evil and can be transferred through the media into ignorant, watching eyes.

What could be cuter than putting Mickey Mouse in a cute little robe with a wand and a huge wizard hat, while directing those wild figures in "Fantasia"? However, one of our New Testament words translated *sorcery* comes from the Greek word *Pharmakeia,* from which we get our word, *pharmacist,* and particularly refers to witchcraft's use of mind-altering drugs. Anything that can enhance Satan's illusion is fair use in his dark kingdom. So is anything he can use to kill. Therefore, witchcraft sorcery also includes various poisons and potions—such as "Adam and Eve" mentioned in chapter 2, which are used to drug victims, cast spells, and kill.

The recent smash movie, "Ghost" (1990), starring Patrick Swayze and Whoopi Goldberg, doesn't seem to hide the devil's agenda in jaded fairytale. It even seems to deal somewhat accurately in the ways of mediums, monthly prognosticators, sorcerors, and palm readers.

The main character in the movie, Patrick Swayze, is killed in an accident, but his spirit gets locked in the cosmos and he is unable to go to heaven or to hell. So, like Saul, he seeks out a practicing witch (medium), Whoopi Goldberg, to communicate with his wife while he is caught between the two worlds.

In one scene, Swayze gets on a train and finds that no one recognizes him. Then he looks up and someone is shouting at him from the train's other end, telling him to get off. As I will discuss more in the next chapter, in every walk of life, there is some type of territorial demon or force that will try to work against us to block the will of God. And in this movie, Swayze actually comes in contact with a territorial demon that controlled the train.

In reality, some territorial spirits will forbid employment to certain ones in their territory, by blocking the minds of individuals. Only the power of the Holy Ghost can destroy the power of territorial demons, which we will look at more closely toward the end of this book.

Why is it important that Satan's puppets produce such programs for unsuspecting audiences? Because, whether his puppets are fully aware of it or not, Satan knows his demons are transferable. He knows the minute something happens in the realm of his demonic, it demands an immediate response—and one of his most effective tricks is to preach his doctrine through staged, media production.

I am not at all confused over all the controversy that is swirling around Disney World's recent sponsorship of homosexual days. Remember, sexual perversion is a fruit of witchcraft, and what better place to flaunt it than in the Magic Kingdom?

"The Simpsons"

Now let's discuss the newest and most insidious of Satan's productions, which is planting his seeds of witchcraft into millions of American homes: "The Simpsons."

Now you say, "Oh, George, 'The Simpsons' is just a cartoon show about a crazy family, so don't try to read witchcraft into that."

"Oh really?" Say that again once you hear me out.

The Simpson family is dysfunctional. You have the mother Marge who is nice and tries to get the family to go church, but Homer just won't go. You have a four-year-old girl who can't walk or talk...who is still in diapers and sucks a pacifier. You have another girl named Lisa who is artistic and very intelligent, and she brings balance to the family. And you have Bart, who draws the most attention.

Bart the Rebel

In the series, Bart's father, Homer, is an idiot. In the opinion of most, there is nothing wrong with being an idiot, but Bart has no respect for his father. He calls him "stupid, idiot, dummy, crazy, and bozo." When there is a rule to be broken or an authority to be mocked, Bart is there to do it in style. And when your child is under the influence of this kind of "entertainment" for thirty minutes, something is taking place.

> *For rebellion is as the sin of witchcraft, and stubbornness is as iniquity and idolatry. Because thou hast rejected the word of the Lord, he hath also rejected thee from being king* (1 Samuel 15:23).

The message this program conveys to our young children in their early impressionable years of molding and shaping is one of rebellion, and the Bible says rebellion is as the sin of witchcraft. So Bart opens up the door at an early age.

Kick Bart Out!

In one episode, Bart is asked by his father to bless the food. So he bows his head, looks up to God, and says, "God, we work hard for everything we have. Thanks for nothing." It was when I watched this that I decided "The Simpsons" was not coming into my house any longer.

Witchcraft is so prevalent that some children are involved in it and don't even know it. Satan can do much with an angry person. And when you enter the demonic realm, Satan installs a revolving door through which he can come and go at will.

America's recent rash of school shootings haven't been carried out by "the Beave" or Eddie Haskall from another generation. They've been carried out by the "Barts" of the 1990s.

Rock Music

Many others have written much on the influence Satan has worked in young people through modern rock music. And this is certainly true. One of the first to openly flaunt their satanic affiliation was a group by the name of KISS (Knights in Satan's Service). Their music in the early '70s was top notch, according to rock standards. But even though they appeared on stage as demonic aberrations, their message was subtle—that is, until they lured you out to a concert. It is said they held actual satanic altar calls after their shows.

Others who followed after KISS became even more overt, and some have been held liable in suicide cases because of parents' claims.

The difference I want to point out between rock and the popular movie media is this—a rebellious teenager may blast his eardrums out with the driving beat of rock to the dismay of his parents, but parents are the ones who often take their children into Satan's world of witchcraft through a rented video or unguarded TV program. Then they wonder why young Barbara has changed her name to Sabrina and is suddenly wearing black lipstick at the age of twelve!

We must take authority over our households and over our children. It must begin with parents, because Satan will corrupt your children right under your noses if you don't control what comes into their eyes and hearts right in your own home.

One of the most popular celebrities on television today is Oprah Winfrey. You have to listen closely, but Oprah also uses her platform to teach and train on the oneness of "I am" or "I have no need for God or any other, because I am." She goes to a universal church in Chicago that doesn't believe in using the blood or the name of the blood. They aren't even allowed to say the word *blood*.

DTV (Demon TV): Witchcraft in the Popular Media

When Oprah talks about "God," she doesn't say Jesus or Jehovah. She speaks about forces, channels, and psychic phenomena.

The other "fool's forums" that have oozed into daytime and very late-night TV popularize the perverse and satanic, often by parading witches and warlocks on stage to confuse viewers with their brand of "truth." Some of them now have witchcraft "experts" (witches) who appear annually around Halloween to present witchcraft's "noble" side of "doing good." But don't write in for their free information brochures because you may get a personal outreach team headed by Beelzebub himself knocking at your door.

You may think I'm making a mountain out of a molehill in pointing out these media truths. But because we are such a media-conscious society, the truth of the matter is, what goes in will come out. This is why television commercials are so powerful. Stop and think about it: when you're out shopping, are you more inclined to purchase a product you saw advertised on TV...or brand X? Tide...or Bartons? Crest...or Millards? You know the power of production is real.

Still, many could blow all of this off as simple entertainment. But don't be deceived. Hollywood has been used to enslave many in the occult. If you were to take a camera into a hundred witches covens today, interview those involved, and ask them what inspired them into the craft, you would be surprised. Television and music would probably top the list.

The plan of Satan is to use the same propaganda over and over again to get us to hear as many of his lies as he possibly can because he knows that sooner or later its going to take root in someone's mind. And when it does, he knows his lie will become their truth. What Satan did once, he will do over and over again—in different centuries, venues, and cultures, but all with the same effect.

The Witching Craft

This is why God's Word is always so powerful, regardless of the time or culture in which it is read and obeyed. When God is honored, witchcraft must bow, and all of hell knows it well:

> *There shall not be found among you any one that maketh his son or his daughter to pass through the fire, or that useth divination, or an observer of times, or an enchanter, or a witch, or a charmer, or a consulter with familiar spirits, or a wizard, or a necromancer. For all that do these things are an abomination unto the Lord:* ***and because of these abominations the Lord thy God doth drive them out from before thee*** (Deuteronomy 18:10-12).

Now let's move on to take a look at where Satan gained his power to control and deceive. Then we will launch into various discussions of God's overcoming power that will terrorize the "terrorist" when His people take the time to believe and obey His Word.

5
Satan Unmasked

But I fear, lest by any means, as the serpent beguiled Eve through his subtlety, so your minds should be corrupted from the simplicity that is in Christ.

—2 Corinthians 11:3

So far we have looked at the earthly origin of astrology and some of the devil's rituals, subtle propaganda, and lusts that propel it. But to get a better understanding of why people would be led to use such practices, we must look at the spiritual roots of witchcraft. And to do this we will turn to the Books of Isaiah and Ezekiel because it is only there that we receive a glimpse of Satan's earliest days.

> *How art thou fallen from heaven, O Lucifer, son of the morning! how art thou cut down to the ground, which didst weaken the nations! For thou hast said in thine heart, I will ascend into heaven, I will exalt my throne above the stars of God: I will sit also upon the mount of the congregation, in the sides of the north: I will ascend above the heights of the clouds; I will be like the most High* (Isaiah 14:12-14).
>
> *...Thus saith the Lord GOD; Thou sealest up the sum, full of wisdom, and perfect in beauty. Thou hast been in Eden the garden of God; every precious stone was thy covering, the sardius, topaz, and the diamond, the beryl, the onyx, and the jasper, the sapphire, the emerald, and the carbuncle, and gold: the*

workmanship of thy tabrets and of thy pipes was prepared in thee in the day that thou wast created. Thou art the anointed cherub that covereth; and I have set thee so: thou wast upon the holy mountain of God; thou hast walked up and down in the midst of the stones of fire.

Thou wast perfect in thy ways from the day that thou wast created, till iniquity was found in thee. By the multitude of thy merchandise they have filled the midst of thee with violence, and thou hast sinned: therefore I will cast thee as profane out of the mountain of God: and I will destroy thee, O covering cherub, from the midst of the stones of fire.

Thine heart was lifted up because of thy beauty, thou hast corrupted thy wisdom by reason of thy brightness: I will cast thee to the ground, I will lay thee before kings, that they may behold thee. Thou hast defiled thy sanctuaries by the multitude of thine iniquities, by the iniquity of thy traffic; therefore will I bring forth a fire from the midst of thee, it shall devour thee, and I will bring thee to ashes upon the earth in the sight of all them that behold thee (Ezekiel 28:12-18).

Satan's Origin

In these passages of Scripture only can mankind find both the origin of Satan and his origination of sin. Sin took root in the spiritual realm when Satan sought to exalt himself above God Almighty.

Isaiah said he was Lucifer, "the bright and shining one" who wanted to exalt his throne above the stars of God.

Ezekiel said he was the anointed cherub (an angel class of being) sealed in the wisdom and beauty of God, that his beauty lifted him up and corrupted his wisdom, and that God cast him to the ground because of his iniquities.

From these scriptures, we can see that Satan was a worshiper and servant of God who rebelled to receive God's worship for himself.

We see Satan attempting this again with Jesus in Matthew 4:5, during Christ's temptation in the wilderness:

> ...*Then the devil taketh him up into an exceeding high mountain, and showeth him all the kingdoms of the world, and the glory of them; and saith unto him, All these things will if give thee, if thou wilt fall down and worship me. Then saith Jesus unto him, Get thee hence, Satan: for it is written, Thou shalt worship the Lord thy God, and him only shalt thou serve.*

Satan took Jesus up to a very high place, just as he led earth's people up in the Tower of Babel in Genesis 11. We can also see that Satan offered Jesus power, wealth, and glory if He would only worship him. Of course, none of what Satan promised Jesus would have ever been fulfilled. Neither do his promises prove true to those who believe and worship him today through the practices of witchcraft, astrology, voodoo, and other wicked acts. Why? Because Satan is a liar. Listen to Jesus' words about him in John 8:44:

> ...*He was a murderer from the beginning, and abode not in the truth, because there is no truth in him. When he speaketh a lie, he speaketh of his own: for he is a liar, and the father of it.*

To those who are foolish enough to follow him in witchcraft, Satan gives just enough power to keep them loyal. But in the end, he kills them and will share their company in the fiery regions of hell.

> *Then shall he say also unto them on the left hand, Depart from me, ye cursed, into everlasting fire, prepared for the devil and his angels* (Matthew 25:41).

In Ephesians 2:2, Paul identifies Satan as the *prince of the power of the air* or the lower atmospheric regions of breathable air (aer). Jude 6 tells us that some of the angels left their *first estate*. And when we think of an estate, we think of a home or dwelling place. So from these passages we can conclude that these angels were ousted from God's holy mount in the third heaven. Most believe they are wandering just above our atmosphere—in *ouranos*, the second heaven—seeking to invade at will where they can.

When Satan attempted to take over heaven, his main motive was to be like the Most High. This means he wanted to receive praise and worship as God did. Since he had communed with God and learned many things, he felt he knew just as much as God did. Lucifer was the brightest angel, but his arrogance blinded him to the fact that God's light was brighter than his. So he ascended above the first heaven, but he didn't realize that God had a third heaven and that his condemnation confined him to the second heaven, where he now resides.

Job reveals Satan as a presence "walking about the earth" (see Job 1:7). So we know that Satan is mobile between heaven and earth. But he is not omnipresent as he would try to have people believe. In other words, he can only be in one place at one time, so he needs his legions of fallen angels to assist him in his cause.

The fallen angels (demons) in Lucifer's kingdom are assigned to certain areas. This can be seen in two passages of Scripture found in Daniel and Ephesians.

> *Then said he unto me, Fear not, Daniel: for from the first day that thou didst set thine heart to under-*

> *stand, and to chasten thyself before thy God, thy words were heard, and I am come for thy words. But the prince of the kingdom of Persia withstood me one and twenty days: but, lo, Michael, one of the chief princes, came to help me; and I remained there with the kings of Persia* (Daniel 10-13).

The prince of Persia is the chief demon assigned to see that evil deeds are carried out on earth in Persia. This demon and his forces of the area see to it that Satan's will is done when men worship them. But when the saints of God begin to pray and bind these forces, God sends forth his angels to war against them to stop their evil deeds.

Ephesians 6:12 gives us the different rankings of the forces of Satan.

> *For we wrestle not against flesh and blood, but against principalities, against powers, against the rulers of the darkness of this world, against spiritual wickedness in high places.*

Ephesians 2:2,3 sheds more light in this area.

> *Wherein in time past ye walked according to the course of this world, according to the prince of the power of the air, the spirit that now worketh in the children of disobedience: among whom also we all had our conversation in times past in the lusts of our flesh, fulfilling the desires of the flesh and of the mind; and were by nature the children of wrath, even as others.*

In this powerful passage, Paul is teaching that before we are born again, the devil controls our actions because his spirits are working in us. But he is much more sophisticated than his lower forms of control would have most people think. When he enslaves a person in the very noticeable practices of Satan worship and witchcraft, many can see his obvious ways. But his highest form of deception comes very subtly and works in more sophisticated ways through "respectable" people and even religion.

Stop and think about it. Men and women in backward collars who oversee congregations in beautiful church buildings and teach against the blood of Jesus are more deadly than voodoo or witchcraft. So are greed-driven businessmen who destroy their competitors. These are much more sophisticated lies. Add to that the crooked politician who says one thing and does another and the oppressive government that abuses human rights—and Satan shines his best, in accepted disguise.

Many who buy into newspaper horoscopes have no idea they are buying into their control by the signs of the stars and that the devils behind the stars are working within them. But one thing can lead to another, and many move up to higher levels of Satan's deception in their quest for spiritual power.

It is when Satan is subtle that he is most dangerous. To make this point, I want to share again the testimony of a woman who was ensnared by a TV psychic hotline. (Also included in my book entitled *Oppressionless*.) Her experience provides a timely revelation of Satan's modern, subtle ways.

Dial 1-900 Psychic, Celebrity TV

I doubt if you have ever called one of these lines yourself or that you will ever call one again once you hear how this woman's innocent desire for hope and information brought Satan into her life.

"One night while up 'channel surfing' on the television, I stumbled upon one of the psychic network shows. I quickly turned away from it, but I turned right back to it because the psychic on the screen had tapped into things that intrigued me. This began a weekly habit of calls, with bills of $10 to $20 per week, which would eventually increase as my desire for more information increased. As time went on, I dialed more and more numbers and paid more and more money, because for me, this meant more in-depth information.

"Finally, at about the third level of my seeking, I heard a very pleasant voice on the other end of the phone that I immediately felt a closeness to. She gave me a strange kind of "knowing" within, and I felt I could trust her with the deepest depths of my inner-most secrets and soulish desires. The psychic's name was Crystal, and as I gave her my time, money, and ear, she told me all there was to know about myself.

"Upon answering my call and introducing herself, Crystal first asked me my date of birth. Then she asked me to repeat my name three times. Ten minutes into the conversation I was hooked. I was totally in awe of things being revealed to her concerning my life. And the accuracy of this woman who just a few minutes earlier was a total stranger astounded me.

"Crystal knew of the fourteen-year-old abused teenager I was when growing up—and of the thirty-three year old who had lost almost everything, including her mind. I had lost my family in a fire that was ruled as arson, and I wanted to know why and who would leave me without a family. I lost my mother, my brother, my husband, and my seven-month-old baby. Depression had set in on my life, and I was about to lose my mind.

"The nightmares were the worst. I dreamed of my husband in the fire, calling out my name, and as I reached for him, he disappeared in the smoke and flames. Watching mothers with their small children became torment for me because I longed to cuddle the baby I'd tragically lost. And although I wanted to mother again, I also longed to be mothered. I longed for someone to provide the same comfort I so missed from my mother.

"So in my desperation to find answers, I was willing to try just about anything that would give me liberty and bring back life as I had once known it.

The Witching Craft

"Crystal provided me with the answers I felt I needed to restore my life. And the more I spoke with her, the more I felt anxiety building up in me to continue speaking with her and gaining her insights. So fascinated and intrigued was I that my heart palpitations increased with excitement, my palms became sweaty as I spoke, and I found myself approaching every new call as an addict going after the next fix.

"Soon, my life revolved around the counsel and direction of Crystal's insight. And before long, I couldn't even consider making a decision without consulting her.

"Crystal eventually told me that by providing her with my phone number she could introduce me to a psychic counselor who could better help me with some of the unanswered questions that still plagued my mind.

Seven Years of Black Magic

"I gladly received Crystal's offer and agreed to make contact with this 'local' psychic counselor. In fact, I was excited, because by now I had become totally engrossed in the mysticism of the psychic realm. My visit would plunge me into seven years of black magic, necromancy, heavy satanic enchantments, praying to ancient spirits, and eventually joining a school for witches, from which I graduated with honors before joining a witch's coven.

"All of this began from a TV psychic hotline that seemed to be so innocent. My minor fascinations with horoscopes, palm readings, or anything mystical that would catch my attention had finally turned into this.

"Once a part of the coven, I learned of a power that I'd never known I had, and I was fascinated by it. I had the power to make people do things against their will, and I loved it! As I progressed, I learned to administer my power of control through spell castings, love potions, hate potions, separation

Satan Unmasked

and accident potions. I could even look into the heart of an individual and tell what they were thinking, then use that information in controlling their lives.

"This practice of oppressive manipulation and witchcraft ruled and reigned in my life for seven years. Then one night, a girlfriend of mine who was one of those born-again, Pentecostal, tongue-talking believers invited me to a tent meeting to hear an evangelist. He was one of those who claimed to have the power of God to cast out demons. At first I declined her invitation. But everyone in town was talking about this man, so I eventually decided to go.

"When the evangelist called me out of the crowd at the meeting, the demon that had taken up residence in my body for seven long years, didn't intend to give up easily. But it was no match against the authority and blood of Christ...and as the man of God prayed and commanded it to come out, I was set free."

The preceding testimony is not only one of deliverance and liberty but it is also a commentary on Satan's deception in one of his most popular, mass-media forms. This woman, whose circumstances drove her to oppressing depression, was also driven to connect with Satan through his deceptive offers of hope.

You may say, "I'd never call one of those numbers," and you probably wouldn't. But this woman did. And so have many others—even within the church. Because its out there on the television set and in magazine ads in soaring numbers, I mention this simply to show oppression's new high-tech psychic outreach, and to warn you about what it can do to a life.

The evangelist who came to this woman's town was me. When I was led to call her forward the night of the meeting, I had no idea of the battle that was awaiting me. Seven years earlier she was lonely and struggling through the horrible tragedy of her family's death, but now she stood before me—

a demonized convert of Satan's lowest order of blatant, open worship. While speaking into her life as the power of God overwhelmed me, this woman's entire countenance and demeanor transformed before my eyes. Her head was bowed down. Then as she slowly lifted it, I could see Satan's hate within her eyes. The demon was letting me know that he had overtaken her and was not going to come out just because I said to do so. Her eyes peered at me with the most gruesome satanic force I had ever seen as the voice of her demon spoke to me:

"YOU come to do war with me, you drug addict?" the demon hissed.

The oppressor sought to oppress me through my failures of my past. And when he did, I'll admit that fear gripped me. But God was in control, and He began to remind me in a powerful way that this fight had nothing to do with me.

So I stood in the authority God had given me, looked this demon right in the face, and proclaimed, "I was once a drug addict—but I am no more. I've been bought by the blood of the Lamb and, in the name of Jesus, I command you to COME OUT!"

Realizing that he was defeated, this demon screeched a horrifying scream and immediately came out of this woman. She is now ministering the Word of God and is being used to bring deliverance to hundreds of people who were bound as she once was. Oppression had bound her in a witches coven, and it all began through a seemingly frivolous TV psychic hotline.

Are you following me? The TV psychic she spoke to separated her from any potential counsel except the psychic counselor who eventually led her to personal contact with a satanic cult.

Satan's Ways Are Subtle

This woman was among those dear people mentioned earlier who are ripe for Satan's picking when they are exposed to the Magic Kingdom and DTV. You may never hear of one of them unless it happens to someone you know...or to a member of your own family. And it probably couldn't be "proven in court" that a Walt Disney movie, watching "Bewitched" and "Night Gallery" fifty-two weeks a year, or listening to a KISS album had anything to do with a child's suicide or a school shooting incident.

This is because Satan's ways are subtle. Ignorance and intrigue are his primary tools. If a person has any knowledge of God's Word at all, Satan will seek to twist its meaning to the point that it becomes of no effect to that person.

"Oh, God's Word is full of grace," he whispers. "You can go into that bar, punch up that pornographic webpage, play around on your wife, deceive your employer—after all, God doesn't know your real needs. And the Bible does say He will forgive you every time."

Then when you lose your job, are run in for drunk driving, or end up in divorce court, the devil sits in the back of the courtroom, laughing at another sucker's demise.

This is what Satan sounds like to Christians who know so little of the Bible that they allow him into the kind of discussions that he had with Eve:

> *...Yea, hath God said, Ye shall not eat of every tree of the garden? And the woman said unto the serpent, We may eat of the fruit of the trees of the garden: but of the fruit of the tree which is in the midst of the garden, God hath said, Ye shall not eat of it, neither shall ye touch it, lest ye die.*
>
> *And the serpent said unto the woman, Ye shall not surely die: For God doth know that in the day ye*

> *eat thereof, then your eyes shall be opened, and ye shall be as gods, knowing good and evil. And when the woman saw that the tree was good for food, and that it was pleasant to the eyes, and a tree to be desired to make one wise, she took of the fruit thereof, and did eat, and gave also unto her husband with her; and he did eat. And the eyes of them both were opened, and they knew that they were naked; and they sewed fig leaves together, and made themselves aprons* (Genesis 3:1-7).

Eve knew so little of God's revealed will that Satan could easily twist her own words against her. Her response to Satan's lie, "We may eat of the fruit of the trees of the garden: but of the fruit of the tree which is in the midst of the garden, God hath said, Ye shall not eat of it, neither shall ye touch it, lest ye die," was only partially true.

God never commanded Adam to abstain from a general tree in the midst of the garden. And He didn't tell Adam not to touch it. What Eve didn't know and Satan sought to twist were these words from Genesis 2:

> *...Of every tree of the garden thou mayest freely eat: but of the tree of the knowledge of good and evil, thou shalt not eat of it: for in the day that thou eatest thereof thou shalt surely die* (Genesis 2:16,17).

God's command was to abstain from eating the fruit of the tree of the knowledge of good and evil. It could have been one of many trees in the midst of the garden. And because there was no command against it, it possibly could have been touched.

The point of the matter is, it was good to obey God's command, and it was evil to disobey. So Satan deceived Eve into disobeying God's command. And he did it with his most popular lie: "Ye shall be as gods" (see Genesis 3:5)

To be a god is to have no other God as the ruler of your own destiny. This is the lie Satan packages and sells most often among those he deceives—generally in the world, and specifically in those who come up to his high place of witchcraft.

Humanism teaches, "There are no other gods besides me." And to "be a god" with supernatural powers is what Satan promises his high-place worshipers following death. Remember, this was the scene painted in the sitcom "Bewitched"—Endora's fellow workers lived on a superior plane as "gods," and from there they could destroy or alter mortals with the wave of a hand.

But it is easy to see that unmasked, Satan is an expert liar at best. He can only draw up to Babel those who believe him on lower ground. In the end, he knows he will be cast into hell, which was prepared for him and his angels (see Matthew 25:41), and in his rage, he seeks to take as many with him as his lying will permit.

So let there be no mistake about it, those Satan can deceive, he can also enslave. Have you ever wondered why the Israelites rebelled so violently against God and Moses when they were led out of Egyptian bondage? Remember, they had witnessed every one of God's supernatural plagues in Egypt, including the parting of the Red Sea, yet when the twelve spies returned with their evil report, they cried out to go "home." Why? Satan was right there in their midst conniving and lying and twisting Moses' words. And he was so effective at it that Joshua and Caleb (who stood firm on God's Word) were the only Hebrews over twenty years old who entered into the promised land.

Today Satan remains masked to the majority of earth's population as he works his ancient ways. Today astrological fortunes are told in daily newspapers and over 1-900 phone lines. Witchcraft can be taken as an elective at certain univer-

The Witching Craft

sities. And Satan's new age religion of sophisticated witchcraft is drawing millions at the highest levels of government as they gather in the halls of power to gaze at crystals, cast their mantra spells, empty their minds through yoga, and engage in sexual perversion at unprecedented levels.

> *But I fear, lest by any means, as the serpent beguiled Eve through his subtlety, so your minds should be corrupted from the simplicity that is in Christ* (2 Corinthians 11:3).

Satan's ways are subtle, until his victims are trapped. It is only then that he reveals his true nature in lower forms of worship in his witching craft.

Of course, the born-again believer who knows the truth of God's Word and has received the power of the Holy Spirit has nothing to fear of the devil, because Jesus said:

> *...I beheld Satan as lightning fall from heaven. Behold, I give unto you power to tread on serpents and scorpions, and over all the power of the enemy: and nothing shall by any means hurt you* (Luke 10:18-19).

Serpents and scorpions are prophetic representations of Satan and his demonic hosts. It was the serpent who tempted Adam and Eve in Genesis 3, and Jesus' connection of them in this passage makes the symbolism complete.

In chapter six, we'll look at some other ways Satan uses his witching crafts to hold people in bondage, sometimes for many generations.

6
Generational Curses and Territorial Spirits

Christ hath redeemed us from the curse of the law, being made a curse for us...

—Galations 3:13

Once while I was in Haiti with a group of people, we were taken to a morgue full of refrigerators, in which bodies lay all over the tables with tagged feet. The undertaker told us that every person in that room was alive. In Haiti, witch doctors are so popular that the religion of the nation is called Obia, which is witchcraft. Obia witch doctors blow dust on their followers, which puts them into a spirit of Zambia, making them Zambies. We were taken to this morgue because this group of Haitians wanted us to go in to pray and break this zambia spell. But I was from America and hadn't yet been taught how to break demonic spells. The only thing I knew was how to preach—and I'm not even sure I had been taught how to do that properly.

So we went inside this eerie place—where I didn't want to be in the first place. I was from New York City, and I wanted to go home! I didn't want to be in a room full of people with the spirit of Zambia on them. Are you kidding? But as we walked into this dark, stench-reeking room, a Haitian man told us, "The last man we brought here to cast off the evil spirits of these people died." Then he asked us to call the evil spirits off these people.

The Witching Craft

Well, I was thinking, *Yo, brother, hey! I'm not the man for this job! Noooo...I've already got a job, thank you.* But there we were, so we started praying to the Father in the name of Jesus.

"Well Lord," we started praying, as we looked around the room, "You said we shall lay hands on the sick and they shall recover, and we shall raise those that are dead."

Suddenly, in the midst of our prayer, we heard a loud thud.

"Ooooh, Lord, let Your blood cover us," were the next words that came out of someone's mouth.

Nobody in the room got up (living or tagged). If they had, I would have been out of there in the blink of an eye. I wouldn't have needed a door either, because you would have seen my body shape in the wall! I knew we were under satanic influence, but I also knew that my training in America had not prepared me for this. So, needless to say, there was no breaking of the Zambia spell that day. But it did open my eyes to the need that existed there.

Most of us here in America have not seen this kind of demon possession. But when you visit Haiti, Africa, or any number of other nations in which witchcraft is a national phenomena, you will get a fast lesson on Satan's manifested power.

Since that experience, I have studied to show myself approved as *a workman that needeth not to be ashamed* (2 Timothy 2:15) when in the presence of Zambi or any other form of Satan's demonic power. Whether it be the drug-induced, spell-casting deceptions of Zambia or the many forms of witchcraft that are practiced in the United States, the first step in dealing with the demonic is spiritual knowledge of Satan's ways.

Many of the demonic strongholds that are prevalent in Haiti and other nations around the world are a result of very visible practices of voodoo and black magic that have been passed down for many generations as a part of their culture. But in America, Satan is much more subtle about it.

The Cure For Generational Curses

The fact that there are generational curses can be seen most openly when children grow up under criminally or cult-driven parents and follow in their footsteps. But generational curses, like Satan, can also be subtle, and we must always be on guard.

Peter admonishes us:

Be sober, be vigilant; because your adversary the devil, as a roaring lion, walketh about seeking whom he may devour: whom resist stedfast in the faith, knowing that the same afflictions are accomplished in your brethren that are in the world (1 Peter 5:8,9).

Notice that Peter said the devil "seeks whom he may devour," not that he "devours whomever he seeks." Again, there is a difference because of our wills.

The reason why the name of Jesus has been fought so hard in the earth is because *there is none other name under heaven given among men, whereby we must be saved* (Acts 4:12). Deliverance from Satan's power will always come to those who believe in the power of God's Word and in Jesus' name. And when a person receives God's forgiveness through the name of Jesus Christ, the subtle lies of the enemy will come to light.

When you take the name of Jesus' and declare war on the enemy (spiritual warfare) there are no peace signings, no retreats, no standoffs. It is a battle unto the death...winner take all. The Bible says, *And from the days of John the Baptist until now the kingdom of heaven suffereth violence, and the violent take it by force* (Matthew 11:12).

The total purpose of attending Bible school, Sunday school, prayer meetings, and Bible studies should be to equip yourself as a member of God's church to do spiritual warfare—learning to wage war on the devil and possess what God has already given us. I certainly could have used such training in my Zambia experience in Haiti. Since that time, I've come to know and preach on the powerful truths of prophesying God's Word in every area of life to destroy the devil's works. Prophesying is when you proclaim, decree, declare, and forecast the things God is going to do in determining your blessing. If it is written in the Word, it is your inheritance in life.

The Bible tells us in Galatians 3:13,14 how any generational curse passed down from generation to generation is broken—through the blood of Christ.

Christ hath redeemed us from the curse of the law, being made a curse for us: for it is written, Cursed is every one that hangeth on a tree: that the blessing of Abraham might come on the Gentiles through Jesus Christ; that we might receive the promise of the Spirit through faith.

This passage tells us that Jesus became a curse for us when He hung on the cross so the Gentiles (all non-Jews) might obtain the blessings of the Lord. The devil may have assigned a territorial spirit, but Jesus became a curse so we could evict him from our lives and be blessed. Jesus became our sin sacrifice by allowing the sins of the world to be laid on His shoulders, so we could become the righteousness of God through Christ. He was wounded so we could be healed. So He took upon himself all the sin of the world with you in mind, thinking He would rather go to hell for you than to go to heaven without you.

Jesus knew we couldn't redeem ourselves from the curse, so he became a curse for us in order to bless us. And when

He did it, He looked down into the ceaseless generations and saw the things that were going to plague our lives.

The works of the flesh Paul lists in Galatians—*Adultery, fornication, uncleanness, lasciviousness, idolatry, witchcraft, hatred, variance, emulations, wrath, strife, seditions, heresies, envyings, murders, drunkenness, revellings...* (Galatians 5:19-21)—are all works the devil is seeking daily to act out in people's lives.

Some who choose to fulfill these lusts end up in prison, in witches covens, or dead. Others make them a regular part of their strife-filled lives and live in daily conflict with others around them in a cursed, miserable existence of spiritual and emotional pain.

Demons Looking for a Place to Dwell

I believe everyone on earth has been assigned a personal territorial demon that takes notes from day one of their lives. Some give these demons more room to express themselves than others, allowing them to build strongholds that control or possess their lives. Entire nations can be controlled to a certain degree when they have government-sponsored witchcraft. Haiti, with it's obia, is a good example.

There are varying views on the actual origin of demons. Some believe they are the disembodied spirits of a pre-Adamic race that lived on the earth between Genesis 1:1 and Genesis 2:2. Others, like myself, believe they are fallen angels who were led astray in Lucifer's rebellion. But one thing is for sure, they need a human body in which to physically express themselves. And they are constantly on the lookout for new "houses"—as Jesus called them—through whom they can manifest.

Jesus disclosed a startling revelation of demonology in Matthew that proves this point.

> *When the unclean spirit is gone out of a man, he walketh through dry places, seeking rest, and findeth none. Then he saith, I will return into my house from whence I came out; and when he is come, he findeth it empty, swept, and garnished. Then goeth he, and taketh with himself seven other spirits more wicked than himself, and they enter in and dwell there: and the last state of that man is worse than the first. Even so shall it be also unto this wicked generation* (Matthew 12:43-45).

In this passage, Jesus pointed out that demons seek to dwell in human bodies and control their actions.

In Luke chapter 5, we see Jesus deliver a man from such a condition.

> *And they arrived at the country of the Gadarenes, which is over against Galilee. And when he went forth to land, there met him out of the city a certain man, which had devils long time, and ware no clothes, neither abode in any house, but in the tombs. When he saw Jesus, he cried out, and fell down before him, and with a loud voice said, What have I to do with thee, Jesus, thou Son of God most high? I beseech thee, torment me not. (For he had commanded the unclean spirit to come out of the man. For oftentimes it had caught him: and he was kept bound with chains and in fetters; and he brake the bands, and was driven of the devil into the wilderness.)*
>
> *And Jesus asked him, saying, What is thy name? And he said, Legion: because many devils were entered into him. And they besought him that he would not command them to go out into the deep. And there was there an herd of many swine feeding on the mountain: and they besought him that he would suffer them to enter into them. And he suffered*

them. Then went the devils out of the man, and entered into the swine: and the herd ran violently down a steep place into the lake, and were choked (Luke 8:26-33).

This man's actions were so controlled by these devils who were possessing his body that he lived naked in a graveyard and continually cut himself with stones (see Mark 5:5).

Now, in this Bible incident, Jesus spoke to the devils. But that doesn't mean that ministering to the demonized should involve similar conversations with demonic beings. Jesus did this under the direction of the Holy Spirit. Why He allowed them to possess the swine was also something He obviously did for reasons we don't understand. Swine were unclean according to Old Testament Law, but there were unexplained reasons for His allowing their possession at the demon's request.

The point of this passage is—this man was possessed by demons and when Jesus commanded them to leave, they had to go! *The deep* they implored the Lord not to send them into is more properly translated, *the abyss.* This abyss is where Satan will be imprisoned as seen in Revelation 20:2.

Again, there are certain people who give their territorially assigned demons the kind of room to grow that eventually allows them to control and even possess their lives. And this was certainly the case with the demoniac of the Gadarenes, as many have come to call him.

Limiting the Devil's Control

However, much more common to the human experience in dealing with territorial sprits are those who give them less authority, but who do submit to their control to a certain degree. It is amazing that some who don't even know Christ can thwart the devil's best efforts in ruining their lives. Why?

The Witching Craft

Because every human being must be willing to submit to the devil's ideas…and some decide not to give in. But many others are not that determined and give in when the enemy comes to persuade them.

There is a spirit behind what we call "peer group pressure," which leads young people astray into unbridled passions, alcohol and drug abuse, and eventually crime. But these young people don't have to submit. The will is always involved. Those who end up in homosexuality submit to Satan's lustful thoughts over and over again, until they believe the lie of their same-sex condition. Those who end up enslaved to alcohol or drugs allow Satan's oppression to bring them to the point of despair, finally buying into substance abuse as a way of escape.

As a young boy growing up on the streets of New York City, I personally succumbed to Satan's lure into drug addiction. My desire to escape the oppressive conditions of my tough neighborhood overrode my desire to resist when offered the temporary escape of drugs. As a result, what began as a "one-time" experience soon evolved into a $270-per-day cocaine habit. So strong was the addiction that I soon began to oppress others in order to satisfy my need. I robbed and stole whatever it took to quench the addiction and find relief.

As I look back today, I can see that God gave His angels charge over me (see Psalm 91:11) in order to get glory from my life. I did go to prison, but I found Christ there.

Today I stand as a living testimony that *if the Son therefore shall make you free, ye shall be free indeed* (John 8:36). I gladly return unto Him a debt that can never be fully paid by preaching His Word all over the world and testifying of His liberating power and authority over every oppressive spirit, including addiction.

When you talk to men or women who end up in prison, most of them have no idea of the role territorial demons had to play in their incarceration. And that old Flip Wilson line, "The devil made me do it," had nothing to do with it. Why? Because the devil can't make anyone do anything. He can only work to influence them.

Those who agree to move up to Satan's high place of promised power and authority, do so because of their proven faith in his lies at the previous level. Before Nimrod agreed to build the Tower of Babel, he was convinced of the importance of the building project. So he launched his campaign based on his belief. But he moved step-by-step in response to Satan's subtle recruitment because this is how the devil works—through a simple lie.

Those caught up in the witching craft end up basing their lives in witchcraft's rituals because they believed Satan's lies at different levels. And you could certainly make a case for full-blown demonic possession in many who the devil enslaves in his craft.

There are others who must deal with the reality of Satan's demons who have no desire to step up to his next level, but at the same time, they don't have very strong wills. There are territorial demons who seek to produce suicide, sexual and substance addiction, unscrupulous businessmen, politicians, and criminal behavior in order to keep people ignorant of any spiritual truth, thus deceiving them into hell. And many die early from lifestyle choices made to seek some relief.

If the will of an individual allows them to resist the gospel truth, then it is enough to fulfill Satan's plan. If he can get people to contribute to his devious will through recruitment at the next level, all the better. But keeping people caught up in his realm of deceit is his overall plan.

Freedom Through the Power of Jesus' Name

But every curse the devil lays on us can be destroyed when the name of Jesus and His Word is applied on the basis

The Witching Craft

of the cross. The woman (mentioned in chapter four) who was drawn into witchcraft through the psychic hotline was totally set free from her demonically invaded life through the power of Jesus' name. If this woman—who had been drawn into the deep things of Satan—had remained in her condition, her life would have been totally different. She may have married again within her coven and raised little witches and warlocks to take her place.

The millions enslaved to Satan on any level of deception could be set free and enter into the liberty of God's Holy Spirit immediately, through the power of Jesus' name. But as it is true that people must accept Satan and his evil ways, people must also accept Jesus. And that's why I've written this book.

When Jesus hung on the tree, He hung suspended between earth and glory until the sun went down—that's the "locking in" of the curse. Then He took us down into the underworld and paid for our sins. And because He did, when we deal with curses, God has given us supernatural power and authority to speak out of our mouths. Curses aren't always dissolved by laying on of hands or sprinkling on oil—many times they are destroyed by what we confess out of our mouths:

> *But what saith it? The word is nigh thee, even in thy mouth, and in thy heart; that is, the word of faith, which we preach; That if thou shalt confess with thy mouth the Lord Jesus, and shalt believe in thine heart that God hath raised him from the dead, thou shalt be saved* (Romans 10:8,9).

Many people's sexual problems date back for many generations—so do their bad teeth, cancer, and alcoholism. Much of the baggage people carry are things other people left as a legacy for them, and Satan holds demonic papers that lay claim to those conditions. A territorial demon simply hangs around a family and claims squatting rights.

In his realm of error, Satan is a legalist. So when he can enslave a person from birth, he will not only do so but will also presume some legal authority in doing it. Of course, God's authority outweighs his. But inherited influences passed down from one generation to another have always been a part of Satan's strategic plan. All strongholds, especially sensual ones that took root early in life, need the redeeming blood of Jesus and His Word to purify and destroy them. So we need to view our deliverance as if we were on trial in a courtroom, which we will do in the next chapter.

7
Court Is In Session

Come now, and let us reason together, saith the LORD: though your sins be as scarlet, they shall be as white as snow; though they be red like crimson, they shall be as wool.

—Isaiah 1:18

Satan's presumption of legal authority rests upon the fact that "he was there first." But anyone who knows the Scriptures knows that's not true. God was first, then came Adam, and then came Satan and his sinful fruit. Looking at it this way, we need to actually sue the devil over certain areas of life and get back the papers of our life. God's Word contains our law of liberty. And Jesus is our lawyer. But it is up to us to file suit.

If you were able to take a look around heaven today, part of what you would see is Lucifer and Jesus in a courtroom. In the courtroom, you would see Jesus who is mankind's advocate as defense attorney. You would see Lucifer who is mankind's prosecuting attorney, because he is the accuser of the brethren. And you would see God as the Judge. I also believe you would see jury seats—each with a drop of Jesus' precious blood which was shed for the remission of our sins.

Satan doesn't lie to God because he knows God is omniscient. So he tells the truth when he is accusing men and women of things they actually did. "He listened to me and did this!" is his basic line of prosecution.

When our Advocate's paralegal comes into the courtroom, Jesus comes alive because His paralegal is the Holy Ghost. And the job of the Holy Ghost is to search all things and bring them to the remembrance of those He defends.

When the saints know heaven's legal system, they understand that the devil's case is thrown out of court every time. Why? Because the devil always burdens his case with inadmissible evidence that he obtains illegally. He never obtains a search warrant. He always breaks and enters to get it. So it is inadmissible.

When you understand the legality of the kingdom of heaven you will stop worrying about many things because the grace of God overlooks them. Whatever we were, the Bible says Jesus became our exchange. When we accept the fact that Jesus is Lord to the glory of God the Father, and when we take captive the devil's lies to the truth of God's royal Law, Satan must hurry out of the courtroom in Jesus name!

To be free from Satan's power, we must learn and understand that God is the law of the first beginning. God is the origin of everything that is good. And we must understand that He is a legalist in the sense that He doesn't do anything illegal or contrary to His law.

But again, as we look at our heavenly courtroom scene, we must also understand that Satan is also a legalist, and that he has certain papers and deeds on your life that he has held since you were in the womb. Across the top of each forged document, it reads, CURSED. And if you don't learn the legal terms of how to get Satan off your back and learn the prophetic truth of God's delivering words that you speak, he will stay there until you die.

Then saith Jesus unto him, Get thee hence, Satan: for it is written, Thou shalt worship the Lord thy God, and him only shalt thou serve. Then the devil leaveth him, and, behold, angels came and ministered unto him (Matthew 4:10,11).

So we need to get a glimpse of what Satan has on us by delving back into our past with the help of our Paralegal Researcher, the Holy Spirit. Then we need to take hold of God's Word, confessing with our mouths and believing with our hearts what God's Word says about us.

Freedom Through the Word of Faith

We having the same spirit of faith, according as it is written, I believed, and therefore have I spoken; we also believe, and therefore speak (2 Corinthians 4:13).

What gets you into fellowship with God? Your confession. What erases your fellowship with God? Your confession. Now, I'm not talking about the power of positive thinking, and I'm not talking about anything that Jesus didn't do himself. You will never hear me promoting anything that Jesus didn't teach in dealing with the devil. So what I'm talking about is the power of the Word of God.

When the even was come, they brought unto him many that were possessed with devils: and he cast out the spirits with his word, and healed all that were sick (Matthew 8:16).

Your mouth is an instrument of power and your heart is an instrument of belief. So when you speak out of your mouth what you believe in your heart, the elements of this earth have to move in your favor.

Words come out of your mouth enclosed in a cage, then they go into your ear, still enclosed in a cage. But after a while, they break out of that cage—and whether they are true words of life or words of death, they will drop into your spirit and control your life.

The Bible teaches that the world responds to the spoken word of faith. And it also declares that God has set before us an open door with a choice to speak and to choose life or death. So it is up to us to choose life.

It is unfortunate that for some people the choice was made for them before they were born through generational curses. But they can be broken through the blood of Jesus and Bible-based spoken words.

What does God's Word say about you? If you say, "I'm broke," then you are broke. Some of us have accepted the fact of being broke. If you walk around confessing that you are ugly, then you are ugly. What you confess will be the plight of your life. What comes out your mouth—accompanied by what you believe in your heart—can cause the powers that govern the earth to move on your behalf.

Because the world responds to the spoken word of faith, Lucifer turned to Jesus and challenged him to ...*command that these stones be made bread* (Matthew 4:3). Lucifer understood the principle, but not enough Christians do. We don't have to just speak positively. So you don't think I'm contradicting myself, let me explain.

There is a difference between painting a totally rosy picture of everything we see, and speaking God's Word of faith. To make this point, there is a story about two boys—an optimistic boy and a pessimistic boy. The optimistic boy was put in a room full of stinking horse manure. The pessimistic boy (probably from the projects) was put in a room filled with brand new toys. Both boys were locked into these places for four hours. At the end of the four hours, when someone went into the room where the pessimistic boy was, they found that he had broken every toy in the room. Then they went into the optimistic boy's room and found him covered from head to toe in horse manure.

Understandably, no one was confused over the pessimistic boy's actions, but they were a little confused over the positive boy's condition. So they asked him why he was playing in the stinking horse manure, and his reply was, "I believed that in all of that horse manure there had to be a horse somewhere."

The moral of the story? Pessimistic people are very optimistic that something is going to go wrong. Optimistic people are optimistic that something is going to go right. So, I believe you need a little of both. You can't crank your car with just two positive cables going to the battery.

Make Your Heavenly Case

But positive, or negative, the enemy wants to make us believe that he has power. And he does. But his power is tied up in heaven's legal system. I could die and leave all of my money to certain people in my family tomorrow. But if other members of my family weren't in agreement with me, they could contest my will in favor of their own. This would then lock up my willed money in the world's legal system, and it would stay locked up until those I left it to could get a good lawyer. Those wanting to alter my legal decision would probably try to prove the unjustness of my choice. But once my heirs got a good lawyer on the case, the legality of my will would win the case.

This is as good a scenario as I can paint to show what actually goes on in the spiritual realm.

God has willed the best He had to offer to those who receive His saving grace. But Satan has contested the will of God, so you have to petition your advocate Jesus to take him on. And Jesus has never lost a case! He will help you get enough of His sacrificial blood smeared on your court papers to get what God says is already yours to use. Just let Him do the talking through His legally recorded Word.

Every time God makes a promise and people tell you, "I thought the Lord was going to do this, that, or the other for you," simply tell them, "It's all right, its just tied up in legalities." The ultimate plan of the devil is to get us to give up. Satan knows that if God doesn't respond quickly to many Christian's prayers, they will give up on Him. He watches when we get up from the altar and between there and the door, we have already asked four or five people for help. So Satan has devised a plan that governs the heavenlies.

Revelation From God

Let me share an experience with you to help prove this point. I came from a hardcore Pentecostal church—which was rough—but I thank God for the discipline. Every Easter night, we would start a fifty-day consecration that lasted from Easter to the Day of Pentecost.

One night—on the fortieth day of one of these fifty-day consecration periods—I had a dream in which I saw the whole world praying. Everything and everybody was praying, and I knew it was the whole world because it was day in some places and night in others.

I also saw a wall in my dream that stretched around the entire world. And when the world would pray, a mist or fog would come out of the mouths of people and go up through the tops of cars and through the ceilings of houses or buildings. It was then that I realized I was up in the heavens.

On top of this wall that encircled the world, I saw demons standing all around the wall. They looked like disfigured animals, and whatever the people were praying they were writing on the wall.

When I woke up, I was shaken by what I had seen because I had really seen something in the heavenly ream. These demonic forces not only knew but were taking note of every one of our prayers! Later on that afternoon, I went to sleep again, and I had the same dream. It was then that I realized it was a divinely imparted revelation of something God was birthing in my spirit.

The revelation was obviously the choice and plan of God because I really didn't consider myself to be a very deep person. He anointed me with this prophetic revelation because He wanted me to come in line with what He wanted me to teach to you.

When I had the second dream I saw a man sitting on a throne with manicured nails and slicked-back hair that came out of his brow. I didn't see his face, only the brow of his forehead. He had an immaculate white suit on and was directing demons with his hand to do different things. I also saw prayers coming out of the saint's mouths that the demons were writing down—again, on these huge walls.

Then I saw an awesome sight. Every so often, an angel would drop down on these demons as they wrote, and they would pull the demons off the walls into a celestial wrestling match. The angels were very overpowering in their strength and stature, and they would throw these ugly creatures up against the wall in police fashion, handcuffing and gagging them. Then I woke up.

Persistent Prayer

These dreams were given to show the saints' great need for persistence—just as Daniel persisted in chapter 10 of his book.

> *Then said he unto me, Fear not, Daniel: for from the first day that thou didst set thine heart to understand, and to chasten thyself before thy God, thy words were heard, and I am come for thy words. But the prince of the kingdom of Persia withstood me*

> *one and twenty days: but, lo, Michael, one of the chief princes, came to help me; and I remained there with the kings of Persia. Now I am come to make thee understand what shall befall thy people in the latter days: for yet the vision is for many days* (Daniel 10:12-14).

The first time I ever laid eyes on these verses was the day God showed me how Daniel's prayer was held up for twenty-one days. I had never heard one sermon on it before I read this passage. I was flipping through the pages of my Bible, and it just shot up off the page. There are wrestling matches going on in the heavenlies when God's saints are praying. And when we persist, we win the day.

Two days after reading this passage, I had another dream. In it, the people of God were praying, but this time I saw what happened to the mist we prayed out of our mouths. I saw the angels in heaven capturing our prayers and running them into God's throneroom.

Angels are amazing beings. What we are allowed to know of them from Scripture shows that they are mighty warriors and faithful messengers. According to Hebrews 1:14, they are servants beings sent forth to minister to the saints. So the enemy knows that every blessing that comes to us must come escorted by angels. He knows that ultimately there has to be a request from earth to the heavenly realm in order to release what God has already given us.

That is why I think this series of dreams was so very important. Everything God has promised is already yours, but until you speak it, the angels can't release it and bring it into being.

> *(As it is written, I have made thee a father of many nations,) before him whom he believed, even God, who quickeneth the dead, and calleth those*

things which be not, as though they were (Romans 4:17).

This scripture tells us to "call those things that be not, as though they were." This means there are things that are supposed to be on the earth that aren't here until you see them in the Spirit and call them into existence.

In context with the Romans scripture quoted above, Abraham was told to change his name from Abram, "Exalted Father," to Abraham, "Father of a Multitude." One year later, Sarah gave birth. Abraham called those things which were not (his fatherhood, "exalted father") into existence because of God's decree.

The same is true for our many promises. They are already there, waiting to be obtained, but they don't know where they belong until we call them home. Satan's evil forces know that every time something is released from heaven, it has to be escorted by angels.

In Revelation 8:3,4, we see the importance of angels with regard to our prayers:

> *And another angel came and stood at the altar, having a golden censer; and there was given unto him much incense, that he should offer it with the prayers of all saints upon the golden altar which was before the throne. And the smoke of the incense, which came with the prayers of the saints, ascended up before God out of the angel's hand.*

As God legislates His authority and his power from heaven, the angels stand ready to take the prayers of the saints from our mouths into God's altar room. There they burn our prayers with incense upon the altar, preparing them as sweet-smelling aromas that ascend into the nostrils of God.

The Lord also knows that when we pray we are attacked by evil forces that try to stop our prayers by sending thoughts

The Witching Craft

to our minds to distract us. So to counter this, He sends angels to protect our minds from every thought that tries to enter. As soon as we finish praying—immediately after we say, "Amen"—I believe angels carry our prayers to the altar room and prepare them to be presented to God.

We have been taught that when we pray, sometimes the answer is "Yes," sometimes "No," and sometimes "Wait." But when we pray in the Holy Spirit, He won't let us pray for something we don't need. So we also need to understand that when we pray in the Spirit, the Holy Spirit helps our infirmities and makes intercessions for us according to the perfect will of God. There is a language in heaven unlike any in the world that only angels can speak and only God can understand. And when we pray in the Spirit, the Holy Ghost comes to our human spirit and speaks through it to get what we need.

But sometimes we simply need to open the door of our house and command Satan to leave. We need to command him out of our children's rooms and pray a protective covering over them.

We must learn to "flip" the curse through the word of our testimony and the blood of the Lamb.

We must learn to praise God through the storm, because we serve a God who *takes us through* until He *brings us out.*

And we must remember that when going through our trials in heaven's court, the fire of our trial will make us foolproof as we stand fast. Satan watches too many get up from the altar and immediately seek human help because of unbelief. But when we stand steady and prove our confession, whatever deceptively cursed situation Satan tries to lie into our lives will prove to be a blessing.

8
Destroying the Power of Witchcraft

> *He that committeth sin is of the devil; for the devil sinneth from the beginning. For this purpose the Son of God was manifested, that he might destroy the works of the devil.*
>
> —1 John 3:8

Witchcraft and astrology have plagued the earth as long as Satan has walked on it. As Solomon said, there truly is nothing new under the sun (see Ecclesiastes 1:9). But because so few understand Satan's deceptions, there are always new revelations from God's Word to help others find their way.

We can see in the Old Testament that God named and forbade witchcraft's well-established practices, which obviously had plagued the nations since Nimrod's Babylonian Tower project around 2300 B.C. And we can see the New Testament apostles confronting it in differing cases.

So in this final chapter, I want to examine more closely what God had to say on the matter in both the Old and New Testaments to give you His final word on utterly destroying the devil's witching craft works.

> *He that committeth sin is of the devil; for the devil sinneth from the beginning. For this purpose the Son of God was manifested, that he might destroy the works of the devil* (1 John 3:8).

Every practice of witchcraft is an abomination unto God because it enslaves innocent people and slanders God's name. As we study the Old Testament, we find that every Hebrew patriarch was at least exposed to the practice, so we also find God's mind on the matter in the Bible's earliest texts.

Abraham was God's vehicle to put man back in contact with the true and living God following Adam and Eve's fall from grace. But it is apparent in Joshua 24:2 that even Abraham himself once worshipped astrology gods:

> *And Joshua said unto all the people, Thus saith the Lord God of Israel, Your fathers dwelt on the other side of the flood in old time, even Terah, the father of Abraham, and the father of Nachor: and they served other gods* (Joshua 24:2).

It is also obvious in Exodus 32 that Abraham's seed learned about astrology and idol worship from the Egyptians during their 430-year captivity. In that chapter, we find the children of Israel making a golden calf (Apis or Taurus) to worship while Moses was on the mountain talking with God. But it is because of Israel's pagan involvements that God revealed His astrological views in the following earliest passages of the Old Testament texts:

> *Thou shalt have no other gods before me* (Exodus 20:3).

> *When thou art come into the land which the Lord thy God giveth thee, thou shalt not learn to do after the abominations of those nations. There shall not be found among you any one that maketh his son or his daughter to pass through the fire, or that useth divination, or an observer of times (astrology), or an enchanter, or a witch, or a charmer, or a consulter with familiar spirits, or a wizard, or a necromancer.*

For all that do these things are an abomination unto the Lord... (Deuteronomy 18:9-12).

For these nations, which thou shalt possess, hearkened unto observers of times (astrology), and unto diviners: but as for thee, the Lord thy God hath not suffered thee so to do (Deuteronomy 18:14).

Ye shall not eat any thing with the blood: neither shall ye use enchantment, nor observe times (Leviticus 19:26).

And the soul that turneth after such as have familiar spirits, and after wizards, to go whoring after them, I will even set my face against that soul, and will cut him off from among his people (Leviticus 20:6).

These earliest passages of Scripture reveal God's views on Satan worship. But as you study the Scriptures closely, you also see how God's power has been resident throughout history to destroy Satan's witching craft.

Moses Versus Pharaoh

When Moses took on Pharaoh's astrologers and magicians, the power of God humiliated them and their dark master in utter defeat.

And Moses and Aaron went in unto Pharaoh, and they did so as the Lord had commanded: and Aaron cast down his rod before Pharaoh, and before his servants, and it became a serpent. Then Pharaoh also called the wise men and the sorcerers: now the magicians of Egypt, they also did in like manner with their enchantments. *For they cast down every man his rod, and they became serpents: but Aaron's rod swallowed up their rods* (Exodus 7:10-12).

When Satan's spirit of rebellion challenged God's established authority, God sent fire from heaven to consume some of Satan's followers and to swallow up the rest in the earth:

They, and all that appertained to them, went down alive into the pit, and the earth closed upon them: and they perished from among the congregation. And all Israel that were round about them fled at the cry of them: for they said, Lest the earth swallow us up also. And there came out a fire from the Lord, and consumed the two hundred and fifty men that offered incense (Numbers 16:33-35).

Elijah Versus Baal

When Elijah confronted the prophets of Baal, God sent fire from heaven to destroy Baal worship in Israel, then empowered his prophet to kill 450 men.

Then the fire of the Lord fell, and consumed the burnt sacrifice, and the wood, and the stones, and the dust, and licked up the water that was in the trench. And when all the people saw it, they fell on their faces: and they said, The Lord, he is the God; the Lord, he is the God. And Elijah said unto them, Take the prophets of Baal; let not one of them escape. And they took them: and Elijah brought them down to the brook Kishon, and slew them there (1 King 18:38-40).

The Hebrew Children Versus Nebuchadnezzar's Court

When Daniel and the other Hebrew children were inducted into Nebuchadnezzar's court, God demonstrated to the king that His power was ten times greater than the power of Satan:

> *And the king communed with them; and among them all was found none like Daniel, Hananiah, Mishael, and Azariah: therefore stood they before the king. And in all matters of wisdom and understanding, that the king inquired of them, he found them ten times better than all the magicians and astrologers that were in all his realm* (Daniel 1:19,20).

In every one of these examples, God destroyed and belittled Satan's powers of astrology to show His superiority over Satan's works in the earth.

Therefore, how much more should we, as God's New Testament Church, be assured of our spiritual power over modern witchcraft in the earth?

But...do we, really? I don't think we do. If we did, every psychic hotline would be out of business, and everyone in witches covens would either turn to the Lord or live in dread of God's powerful local church.

The spiritual warfare rights and power of attorney we have received in Jesus' name will destroy the devil's works. But they must be applied in faith to release God's superior power into our daily fight.

Now, I know there aren't many of us who are "there"—walking in that place of proper authority. So please don't take my last few statements in a condemning way. Rather, take them as an opportunity to grow in faith. As we complete this book by looking at the delivering power of God's Holy Spirit that was released in His earliest church, I believe it will inspire and equip us to destroy Satan's work by faith today.

Philip, Peter, and John Versus Simon

Witchcraft was a huge cultural phenomenon in the earliest days of the church as recorded in Acts. When the church was *...scattered abroad throughout the regions of Judaea and Samaria...* (Acts 8:1), the evangelist Philip started a crusade in the city of Samaria.

Samaria was the city where the wicked queen Jezebel instituted Baal worship in Israel (see 1 Kings 16:24-32). Elijah destroyed her prophets and mocked Satan's worship nine hundred years before Philip brought the gospel into the city. But by the time Philip arrived, Satan's witchcraft had re-rooted and many of its people were under curses or spells. It was also in Samaria that Simon the sorcerer—as mentioned in my introduction—had control of this city through his magic powers. That is, until Philip, then Peter and John were sent.

> *Then Philip went down to the city of Samaria, and preached Christ unto them. And the people with one accord gave heed unto those things which Philip spake, hearing and seeing the miracles which he did* (Acts 8:5,6).

Many of Samaria's people were in the captivity of demons. So the first thing Philip let them know was that Jesus came to set them free. He may have preached from Isaiah 61:1—*...He hath sent me to bind up the brokenhearted, to proclaim liberty to the captives...* But Philip didn't just come with a "message." No, he came with the power of God to show them God's reality.

The result?

> *For unclean spirits, crying with loud voice, came out of many that were possessed with them: and*

many taken with palsies, and that were lame, were healed (Acts 8:7).

The gospel lifts people with the knowledge that Jesus came to give man God's abundant life, while at the same time revealing that Satan comes to steal, kill, and destroy people's lives (see John 10:10).

After the Spirit of God delivered many from demon possession and physical sickness, Satan's head astrologer in Samaria, Simon the sorcerer, came to find out about this power that was greater than his:

> *But there was a certain man, called Simon, which before time in the same city used sorcery, and bewitched the people of Samaria, giving out that himself was some great one* (Acts 8:9).

Simon—like so many psychics parading around American TV airwaves today—puts on an air of spirituality. And since the people were ignorant of the true and living God, they didn't understand the source of Simon's power. So they feared him.

> *To whom they all gave heed, from the least to the greatest, saying, This man is the great power of God. And to him they had regard, because that of long time he had bewitched them with sorceries* (Acts 8:10,11).

Simon Lives

Things haven't changed. There are many Simon's among us today who are accepted and revered by many as representatives of God. But as we study God's Word, we can discern the charlatans from God's true messengers. Bondage and control are too common in the church today—and this is one modern-day Simon "give-away sign." So is "charging" to pray for the sick. A word to the wise is sufficient.

Once Simon saw the demonstration of God's power and received the gospel, he also believed and was baptized. Then when Peter and John came down from Jerusalem to minister the baptism of the Holy Spirit to Samaria's converts, Simon sought to *buy* God's power. But when he did, Peter rebuked Simon's gall and iniquity, driving the new convert in prayer to his knees, saying, *Pray ye to the Lord for me, that none of these things which ye have spoken come upon me* (Acts 8:24).

Paul Versus Elymas

When Elymas the sorcerer opposed Paul on the Island of Paphos, the Spirit of God struck the sorcerer blind, according to Paul's words:

> *And when they had gone through the isle unto Paphos, they found a certain sorcerer, a false prophet, a Jew, whose name was Bar jesus: which was with the deputy of the country, Sergius Paulus, a prudent man; who called for Barnabas and Saul, and desired to hear the word of God. But Elymas the sorcerer (for so is his name by interpretation) withstood them, seeking to turn away the deputy from the faith.*
>
> *Then Saul, (who also is called Paul,) filled with the Holy Ghost, set his eyes on him, and said, O full of all subtlety and all mischief, thou child of the devil, thou enemy of all righteousness, wilt thou not cease to pervert the right ways of the Lord? And now, behold, the hand of the Lord is upon thee, and thou shalt be blind, not seeing the sun for a season.*
>
> *And immediately there fell on him a mist and a darkness; and he went about seeking some to lead him by the hand. Then the deputy, when he saw what was done, believed, being astonished at the doctrine of the Lord* (Acts 13:6-12).

Destroying the Power of Witchcraft

Paul was doing God's will when he encountered this practitioner of witchcraft—and when he did, the Holy Spirit empowered his words. Never forget that! Never forget the power of your confession when it is based in God's sovereign will. Sergius Paulus, the island's governor, repented of his sin as he witnessed this power of God.

Paul and Silas Versus the Craft

When Paul and Silas ministered in Philipi, they met a woman possessed with a spirit of divination. Remember, divination is the practice of using the stars and evil spirits to foretell the future:

> *And it came to pass, as we went to prayer, a certain damsel possessed with a spirit of divination met us, which brought her masters much gain by soothsaying: The same followed Paul and us, and cried, saying, These men are the servants of the most high God, which show unto us the way of salvation. And this did she many days. But Paul, being grieved, turned and said to the spirit, I command thee in the name of Jesus Christ to come out of her. And he came out the same hour. And when her masters saw that the hope of their gains was gone, they caught Paul and Silas, and drew them into the marketplace unto the rulers* (Acts 16:16-19).

This fortune teller, as we would call her today, worked for a group of men who marketed her services. But when Paul recognized her true mission in dogging his tracks, he cast the evil spirits from this woman so she could no longer cast spells. How? Through the gift of the *discerning of spirits* (1 Corintians. 12:10) and the power of Jesus' name. Once he detected the woman's demonic disturbance, he declared, "I command thee in the name of Jesus Christ to come out of her!" And the woman was free.

The Witching Craft

These kinds of demonic disturbances aren't all that uncommon in many churches today. When leaders aren't sensitive to the Holy Spirit, Satan's agents can destroy our ability to go forth with God's Word. But if we are led by the Spirit of God, we can bind and cast these spirits out, as Paul did—in Jesus' name!

Paul Versus "The Book of Shadows"

When Paul entered the city of Ephesus, the ministry of the Holy Spirit was so powerful in destroying the strongholds of witchcraft that—*many of them also which used curious arts brought their books together, and burned them before all men...* (Acts 19:19).

It was in Ephesus that the witch doctors of Paul's day realized that what he was doing was greater than anything they had ever witnessed. In their observations, they noticed he didn't use potions, charm bags, or sacrifices. And they were stunned by the power of Jesus' name. As a result, a group of seven local men decided to try to cast out demons by trying to imitate what Paul did—and they were beaten bloody for their efforts:

> *Then certain of the vagabond Jews, exorcists, took upon them to call over them which had evil spirits the name of the Lord Jesus, saying, We adjure you by Jesus whom Paul preacheth. And there were seven sons of one Sceva, a Jew, and chief of the priests, which did so. And the evil spirit answered and said, Jesus I know, and Paul I know; but who are ye? And the man in whom the evil spirit was leaped on them, and overcame them, and prevailed against them, so that they fled out of that house naked and wounded. And this was known to all the Jews and Greeks also dwelling at Ephesus; and fear fell on them all, and the name of the Lord Jesus was magnified* (Acts 19:13-17).

It appears that the demonic possession of this man in Ephesus gave him strength similar to that of the demoniac of the Gadarenes, which we looked at in chapter six. These seven sons of Sceva were beaten until they were bloody and naked by this demon possessed man because they obviously had no right to use the name of Jesus. They weren't born again and didn't know God's power, so they used the name of Paul—"We adjure you by Jesus whom Paul preacheth..."—with horrible results.

Until we accept the Lord Jesus into our hearts, we aren't part of God's kingdom. This was the bad news for Sceva's sons. But it is good news for every one of us who have received the grace and power of the Holy Spirit and who have inherited the right to use Jesus' name.

So, again the Apostle Paul teaches us to confront and destroy the power of witchcraft through faith in Jesus' name.

> *Behold, I give unto you power to tread on serpents and scorpions, and over all the power of the enemy: and nothing shall by any means hurt you* (Luke 10:19).

> *And these signs shall follow them that believe; In my name shall they cast out devils (evil spirits)...* (Mark 16:17).

A look at the end results of Paul's Ephesus ministry proves again the complete superiority of God's power over the deceptions of witchcraft, when wielded in New Testament faith:

> *And many that believed came, and confessed, and showed their deeds. Many of them also which used curious arts brought their books together, and burned them before all men: and they counted the price of them, and found it fifty thousand pieces of*

silver. So mightily grew the word of God and prevailed (Acts 19:18-20).

The books that were burned in the town square at Ephesus probably included their *Book of Shadows*. This was a witchcraft book that contained everything Satan's followers had learned about sorcery and magic over the previous 2,300 years. So this was Ephesus' way of saying that God's power and the name of Jesus was greater than anything Satan had to offer.

Hell's Response

These accounts in the Book of Acts not only serve to show us the power God has invested in His church but to destroy Satan's works. They also give us a look at what happens when the demonic hosts of witchcraft are confronted by the power of God. So in concluding this book, let's look at how hell responded to Christ's destruction of Satan's witchcraft operations, and then consider your call in the church.

First, when Satan's enterprises are destroyed by God's power, Satan always persecutes the vessels who released God's power.

Paul and Silas were thrown into jail after delivering the woman in Philipi.

When Peter released the Holy Spirit's signs and wonders in Acts 5, he was persecuted by a religious group—the Sadducees.

Stephen preached against the astrology behind Israel's idolatry in Acts 7, and he was stoned to death.

> *And they made a calf in those days, and offered sacrifice unto the idol, and rejoiced in the works of their own hands. Then God turned and gave them up to worship the host of heaven* (astrology); *as it is written in the book of the prophets...*

> *When they heard these things, they were cut to the heart, and they gnashed on him with their teeth.... Then they cried out with a loud voice, and stopped their ears, and ran upon him with one accord, and cast him out of the city, and stoned him...* (Acts 7:41,42,54,57,58).

Following Paul and Silas' tremendous success in Ephesus, they were eventually forced to leave because an idol-maker by the name of Demetrius stirred up the business community:

> *For a certain man named Demetrius, a silversmith, which made silver shrines for Diana, brought no small gain unto the craftsmen; whom he called together with the workmen of like occupation, and said, Sirs, ye know that by this craft we have our wealth. Moreover ye see and hear, that not alone at Ephesus, but almost throughout all Asia, this Paul hath persuaded and turned away much people, saying that they be no gods, which are made with hands: so that not only this our craft is in danger to be set at nought; but also that the temple of the great goddess Diana should be despised, and her magnificence should be destroyed, whom all Asia and the world worshippeth.*
>
> *And when they heard these sayings, they were full of wrath, and cried out, saying, Great is Diana of the Ephesians. And the whole city was filled with confusion: and having caught Gaius and Aristarchus, men of Macedonia, Paul's companions in travel, they rushed with one accord into the theatre. And when Paul would have entered in unto the people, the disciples suffered him not. And certain of the chief of Asia, which were his friends, sent unto him, desiring him that he would not adventure himself into the theatre....*

> *And after the uproar was ceased, Paul called unto him the disciples, and embraced them, and departed for to go into Macedonia* (Acts 19:24-31;20:1).

From these examples, we can understand why many preachers don't preach against witchcraft, cast out devils, or lay hands on the sick in America today. "Those things only happened in the Bible days," they tell their congregations, "and miracles aren't for today." These are doctrines of the devil, which he continues to use today in his evil quest to enslave more people.

And while many churches seem happy to build bigger buildings and send missionaries thousands of miles away, the witching craft in America is growing larger and more popular every day.

The world is falling prey to Satan's witchcraft via psychic TV hotlines every hour.

Our movies and television programs continue to serve as Satan's subtle pulpits of deceit.

Many of God's beloved saints are bound in demonic deception and ignorantly accept it.

But Jesus died to destroy these works—so what are you going to do?

It's Time To Act!

To those of my brethren who have fallen prey to Satan's doctrines of deceit and have hidden out from the battle, I say—it is time to ACT on the Word of God. It is time to learn how to pray.

The Book of Acts is called the Acts of the Apostles. So now is the time for us to follow suit. Satan may work through human beings to come against us—and if that happens, we must stand on God's Word, which says:

No weapon that is formed against thee shall prosper... (Isaiah 54:17).

Like the apostles, we as Christians have the same gift and ability—through Christ—to cast out devils and destroy Satan's works (see Acts 1:8). But again, we must believe it and go to work.

As saints of the most high God, we should know that the hand of God is always with us. We must allow our prayers to ascend into heaven as incense everyday. And we should pray for, support, and exhort others who stand up against Satan and his demonic kingdom.

Remember, Satan works under the cover of darkness through deceptive disguises and fairytale facades. His witching craft works to enslave men's souls in shadowy, subtle ways. This is why Paul wrote: *But all things that are reproved are made manifest by the light: for whatsoever doth make manifest is light* (Ephesians 5:13).

Strike a match in a dark room and light overpowers the darkness. Likewise, let us preach truth in our churches, over our airwaves, and in the streets. When Satan's witching craft appears in our culture, let us call God's angels into the fight to establish His ways. Let us awake from our neglect and shout out the deceit of Satan's subtle ways. The power of Christ will destroy Nimrod's new towers, but we—His born-again church—must light the way with the fullness of God's Spirit and the brightness of His truth.

Pray this prayer with me now:

Father, I thank You because Your power is greater than all the evil plans of the enemy. And in the name of Jesus, I determine this day to stand up against the witching crafts that are running rampant in our land today. I ask You to help me as I endeavor to share with others the subtle deceitfulness of Satan's evil plan and point them to Your saving and delivering power. I ask You to anoint me with Your power as I seek to bring light and truth into the darkness of the devil's demonic kingdom. In Your name I pray, and I'll give You all the glory. Amen.

G.G. BLOOMER MINISTRY PRODUCTS

BOOKS

I'm Not Who You've Heard I Am	$5.95
Oppressionless	8.99
When Loving You Is Wrong But I Want To Be Right	11.99
Witchcraft In the Pews Who's Sitting Next to You	10.99
101 Questions Women Ask About Relationships	7.99

AUDIO CASSETTES

Shaking the Poison Loose	$5.00
Demons & How They Operate	5.00
The Witch Is Dead	5.00
Something Big	5.00
Foolish People	5.00
Jesus Sees You From Where He Is	5.00
Preparation Precedes Blessing	5.00
I'm Not Who I Told You I Was	7.00
It's the Law	7.00
NOW How Are You Going To Get Home?	7.00
The Tomb Is Empty	7.00
Be Eagle Minded	7.00
Saved, Being Saved, Going To Be Saved	7.00
If It Hasn't Come, It Will Come	7.00
Mr. Goodbar	7.00
God's Purpose For Time	7.00

You've Got What It Takes To Be Delivered 7.00
Noise, Bones, Breath, Shaking & Spirit 7.00
Apples & Oranges (2-part series) 15.00
Breaking Generational Curses (2-part series). 15.00
Breaking the Spirit of Poverty (2-part series). 15.00
Engaged in Spiritual Warfare (3-part series). 15.00
God's Been Good To Us (2-part series). 15.00
It's Mess That Makes You (2-part series) 15.00
Preparation Precedes Blessing (3-part series) 15.00
You Can Never Outgive God (2-part series) 15.00
KNOW Your Place (4-part series) 20.00
Witchcraft In the Pews (3-part series) 20.00

VIDEOS

Anointed Trio $15.00
Be Eagle Minded. 15.00
Breaking Generational Curses 15.00
But Elijah Is At the Gate. 15.00
God's Purpose For Time. 15.00
I'm Not Who I Told You I Was 20.00
It's Mess That Makes You. 20.00
Man In The Mirror 20.00
NOW How Are You Going To Get Home 20.00
Take the Keys and Unlock the Door 15.00
The Tomb Is Empty 20.00
Warning, Angels In Charge. 20.00
What Seal Is On Your Relationship? 15.00
Witchcraft In the Pews. 25.00

G.G. BLOOMER MINISTRIES
ORDER FORM

Title	Unit (Please check one)	Price	Qty.	Total
_____	☐ Book ☐ Tape ☐ Video	_____		
_____	☐ Book ☐ Tape ☐ Video	_____		
_____	☐ Book ☐ Tape ☐ Video	_____		
_____	☐ Book ☐ Tape ☐ Video	_____		
_____	☐ Book ☐ Tape ☐ Video	_____		
_____	☐ Book ☐ Tape ☐ Video	_____		
_____	☐ Book ☐ Tape ☐ Video	_____		

TOTAL BEFORE SHIPPING _____

SHIPPING & HANDLING **2.00**

TOTAL ENCLOSED _____
(including Shipping & Handling)

SHIP TO:

Name _____

Address _____

City _____ State ____ Zip _____

Phone (___) _____

Make checks payable to: G. G. Bloomer Ministries

MAIL TO: G. G. BLOOMER MINISTRIES
P.O. BOX 11563
DURHAM, NC 27703

Please allow 2-4 weeks for delivery. THANK YOU!

Notes

Notes

Notes

Notes

Notes

Notes